AF316776

Divine-Human Encounter

Divine-Human Encounter

The Path to God in the Thought of
Abraham Joshua Heschel

HAROLD KASIMOW

Foreword by Maurice Friedman

*Edited and with an introduction
by Jo-Ann Mort*

WIPF & STOCK · Eugene, Oregon

DIVINE-HUMAN ENCOUNTER
The Path to God in the Thought of Abraham Joshua Heschel

Wipf & Stock
An Imprint of Wipf and Stock Publishers
199 W. 8th Ave., Suite 3
Eugene, OR 97401

www.wipfandstock.com

PAPERBACK ISBN: 979-8-3852-1142-5
HARDCOVER ISBN: 979-8-3852-1143-2
EBOOK ISBN: 979-8-3852-1144-9

VERSION NUMBER 04/22/24

We dedicate this book to the people across the
world who have been inspired by Rabbi Abraham
Joshua Heschel to help heal our planet.

Contents

Foreword
(from the 1979 edition)

Because of my thirty-year friendship with Abraham Joshua Heschel and my own great interest in his thought, and because of my friendship with Harold Kasimow, it is a double pleasure for me to write a foreword to his book *Divine-Human Encounter: The Path to God in the Thought of Abraham Joshua Heschel*. I was the chairperson of the doctoral dissertation for the Department of Religion at Temple University on which this book is based, and I myself spoke with Professor Heschel several times about the work that Professor Kasimow was doing on his thought. Heschel was pleased with it because Kasimow brought a full knowledge of Heschel's Hebrew and Yiddish writings as well as his English and German ones. *Divine-Human Encounter* is, in fact, the first full-length scholarly study to be published on Heschel's thought, the only other book being Franklin Sherman's little *The Promise of Heschel* and beyond that a great many articles and essays, including my own lengthy monograph on "Abraham Joshua Heschel: The Philosopher of Wonder," published only in Hebrew. Harold Kasimow had studied for a year with Heschel at the Jewish Theological Seminary in 1957–58. Now, in preparation for his dissertation, he went back again, commuting to New York from Philadelphia once a week and spending the day after the rabbinical seminar in Heschel's office where he was able to peruse Heschel's vast library, see any number of Heschel's own works in various stages of production, see Heschel's correspondence concerning his dialogue with Eastern religions, and, of course, enjoy many hours of fruitful conversation with Heschel himself.

The publication of the first scholarly book on Heschel is long past due. Since Heschel's death at the end of 1972 the interest in his thought on the part of Jewish and non-Jewish scholars alike has grown steadily in America and throughout the world. Yet nowhere has a definitive study been available that could serve as "a guide to the perplexed"; for many readers, even those of a philosophical and scholarly bent, have been puzzled by Heschel's style and his progression of thought, proceeding as they do more insight by insight than logical link by logical link, dazzling in the richness of their imagery, and, often as not, conditioned by counter-emphasis, which was part and parcel of the polarity of Heschel's thinking. The logical structure in Heschel's writings is not easily perceptible, because his style is poetic and his philosophy mystical and in-tuitive. The difficulty is further increased by the fact that Heschel's thought is dialectical and even paradoxical in nature. Although his individual insights have value in themselves, none of them can be taken as expressing the whole of his philosophy. As a result, it is difficult to grasp the total import of his thought. "Polarity is an essential trait of all things," Heschel wrote. Jewish prayer, for example, is guided by the opposite principles of "order and outburst, regularity and spontaneity, uniformity and individuality, law and freedom, a duty and a prerogative, empathy and self-expression, insight and sensitivity, creed and faith, the word and that which is beyond words."

The polarity of Heschel's thought, the mosaic of individual insights, and the tendency to stress now one point of view and now another—all these make the task of the responsible interpreter and critic a difficult one. The reader of Heschel's works will avoid much misunderstanding if he will look, in the first instance, not for a system but for central insights, and then move outward from these insights to the structure of Heschel's thought. This structure might better be compared to the concentric circles that are produced when a stone is thrown into a pool than to the precise architectonic that one finds in more systematic philosophies of religion. For this reason, it is essential that we suspend any final conclusions about Heschel's thought until we have seen not only the stone falling into the pool but the outermost concentric rings.

The great virtue of Harold Kasimow's *Divine-Human Encounter* is that he enables us to see both the stone being thrown and the outermost concentric circles. He does this, in the first instance, through a study of the influences on Heschel's thought, particularly the Jewish mystical (Hasidic) ones, that has never, to my knowledge, been attempted before, and, in the second, through a clear organization of Heschel's insights according to the tripartite path to God that Heschel himself set forward in his single most impressive study of the philosophy of Judaism—*God in Search of Man*: the path to God through the world, through the Hebrew Bible, and through the "holy dimension" of sacred deeds and sacred living in the everyday world. Finally, Kasimow not only traces for us the significant meeting points between Heschel and Christian thought, both Protestant and Catholic, which have already had a great impact in our time, but also extrapolates the as yet only very partially realized dialogue between Heschel and Eastern thought, to which Professor Kasimow brings the background of a profound understanding of Hinduism, Buddhism, Zen, and Islam.

For all these reasons, the publication of Harold Kasimow's *Divine-Human Encounter* is an occasion to be welcomed by scholars in many fields and by intelligent laymen concerned with religion, philosophy, and that sense of wonder, or awareness of the ineffable, which Heschel held to be "the root of man's creative activities in art, thought, and noble living."

Maurice Friedman
Solana Beach, California
December 1978

Preface

A FEW WEEKS BEFORE he died in 1972, my teacher, Abraham Joshua Heschel, told an NBC interviewer that young people must "remember that the meaning of life is to build a life as it if were a work of art."[1] Heschel's life was a masterpiece. He was one of the most significant thinkers of the last century, who was also deeply engaged in the social issues of his day. He was a passionately committed Jew—considered a tzaddik by Jews. He was an "apostle to the gentiles" and was also revered by many Christians.

Heschel was a major figure in the social change movements of his day—to end the Viet Nam War and to support the Civil Rights Movement. He worked vigorously to help Jews suffering in the Soviet Union.

What made Heschel unique at the time was his insistence that a Jew should communicate as a Jew but reach beyond the boundaries of his own religious tradition. The Catholic theologian John Merkle said it best: "In his own life and works, Abraham Joshua Heschel revealed the supreme importance of God as well as what it was like to live with faith in God."[2] Indeed, Heschel played a major role in shaping the Catholic Church's view of Judaism. He was the most important Jewish voice during the meeting of the Second Vatican Council in the 1960s.

1. Heschel in "Carl Stern's NBC Interview with Dr. Heschel," quoted in Heschel, *Moral Grandeur and Spiritual Audacity*, 412.

2. Merkle, *Genesis of Faith*, 26.

This book aims to clarify the ideas of this great Jewish scholar by placing them within a systematic framework. Since the original publication of this book, in 1979, there has been a revival of Heschel's legacy and his ideas. His particular perspective of a "path to God" has been traversed by Jewish and non-Jewish scholars alike and by activists inspired by his vision of God's investment in humanity.

I will bring greater coherence to the major works of Heschel, dividing this pathway to God in three main paths. As Heschel wrote: "There are three starting points of contemplation about God; three trails that lead to him. The first is the way of sensing the presence of God in the world, in things; the second is the way of sensing His presence in the bible; the third is the way of sensing His presence in sacred deeds."[3]

Heschel's major work, *God in Search of Man*,[4] has been called "the single most sophisticated, profound, and comprehensive statement within modern Judaic theology."[5] This book explores Heschel's three interrelated pathways through which a contemporary person can experience God, or more precisely, how a person can respond to a God who is indeed searching for partnership with each of us.

Most of his other major works are devoted primarily to one of the three categories he first outlined in this work. *Man Is Not Alone* is concerned with the first aspect of the path, the way to God via the world. *The Prophets* and *Theology of Ancient Judaism* are devoted to the second aspect, the way to God through the Bible. Heschel's *Man's Quest for God* is largely given to the third aspect, the way to God through sacred deeds.

This book will illustrate how Heschel's thought uses these three pathways as an organizing principle, creating a balance between the rational and mystical poles of the Jewish tradition.

---

3. Heschel, *God in Search of Man*, 31. Cited hereafter as *GSM*.

4. I will try to be more gender inclusive in writing here, but Heschel, a person of his time, uses the word "man" to represent a person regardless of their gender and, due to the material, I will mostly rely on his usage.

5. Friedman, "Abraham Joshua Heschel: Philosopher," 12.

An examination of Heschel's thinking will reveal that he is an authentic Jewish voice who indeed presents an accurate Jewish theology. This analysis will also reveal how each aspect of his path has important implications for Christianity. I will clarify Heschel's most fundamental presuppositions. They are not always fully developed. At times, they seem inconsistent with his own theological structure.

I will bring his most essential ideas into dialogue with his most important critics. Here, I will examine the criticism of Heschel by four important Jewish thinkers—Eliezer Berkovits, Marvin Fox, Maurice Friedman, and Jakob Petuchowski.

Each aspect of Heschel's path is essentially "a way of developing sensitivity to God and attachment to His Presence."[6] It is especially important to show how Heschel's authentically Jewish writings have made a profound impact on the Christian world. Heschel remains the most significant Jewish thinker to address the issue of religious diversity, arguing that no religion has a monopoly on truth or holiness. He writes that "diversity of religions is the will of God."[7] It is an extremely important contribution that I believe can continue to lead to a genuine and productive dialogue between Judaism and Christianity.

Additionally, Heschel's ideas open the door to dialogue with more distant religious traditions. Although Heschel's ideas sometimes contrast radically with Asian thought on many ultimate issues, nevertheless, as we will see, his ideas make possible an honest and open communication between Judaism and Asian thought. As Jewish and Asian thought gets closer through the ages, this aspect of Heschel is increasingly important and groundbreaking. Heschel was very much in love with the Jewish tradition, but his greatness lies in his ability to recognize the humanity and touch of divinity present in other religions.

I begin the book with an examination of the major influences on Heschel's thought, stressing how his theology has been

6. Heschel, *GSM*, 26.

7. Heschel, "No Religion Is an Island," 14.

influenced by Hasidic thought. Heschel's treatment of Hasidism provides insight into many of his most fundamental ideas.

Harold Kasimow
Grinnell College
Grinnell, Iowa
2023

Acknowledgments

First and foremost, I wish to express my deep gratitude to Jo-Ann Mort, a talented student in my first class on the work of Abraham Joshua Heschel back in 1972, for her excellent revision of this book, originally written as a PhD thesis for Temple University and published in 1979 by University Press of America. All these years later, with this new version of the book, Jo-Ann has given us deeper and clearer insight into Heschel's thought and has made this book more readable for a wider public. Jo-Ann and I are happy to acknowledge our unending gratitude to Rabbi Heschel, who immeasurably enriched each of our lives. My gratitude also goes to my students for deepening my understanding of Heschel's work and to my family, my friends, my teachers, and my colleagues who, over the years, have blessed and encouraged me to continue exploring the wisdom of Heschel.

Introduction

I FIRST MET HAROLD Kasimow in 1972. I was sixteen years old and a confirmation student at Rodeph Shalom, the largest Reform Congregation in Philadelphia, Pennsylvania. Harold was one of my teachers. We studied Abraham Joshua Heschel's book *The Earth Is the Lord's*. I still have my copy of that book from class, scribbled with notes of exploration and discovery.

To say that Harold's introduction of Heschel to my teenage mind was influential for my future path is honestly a great understatement. Studying Heschel with him, and discovering Heschel, propelled me on a path toward a life that I have tried to live with Jewish values and engagement, regarding my home here in America and my love for Israel. Heschel has always been my guide.

Heschel spoke to my yearning, within a Reform Jewish framework, for a Judaism that was spiritual yet connected to social justice, respectful of the past, but targeted to the future. At that time, Reform Judaism hadn't transformed itself into a movement embracing more Hebrew and prayerful engagement. The congregation I attended was established in Philadelphia in 1795 as the first Ashkenazi congregation in the Western Hemisphere. There was a vast membership—our confirmation class had ninety-three students in it. The historic sanctuary was both majestic and foreboding, with a choir who sang the prayers from a space hidden behind the arc as we all stood in silence, listening, observing, not participating. I knew that I yearned for something more.

It was hard to feel that religious learning was intimate in a setting such as this, but Heschel—and Harold Kasimow's interpretation of Heschel—made it a lifelong experience. I was taken by Heschel's teachings because they brought me deeper along in my own Jewish journey.

The influence of Heschel on the Reform Movement of Judaism as well as on other contemporary Jewish streams is profound. Indeed, Reform Judaism transformed as the years went on—and I would postulate that Heschel influenced that change toward more religiosity and spirituality. Today, Heschel's teachings are heard regularly from Reform pulpits, and studied intensely by Reform clergy and other students.

Most importantly, his dictum to "pray with our feet," as he said when he spoke out against the Viet Nam War, or when he marched in Selma, Alabama, with Dr. Martin Luther King Jr., speaks to many Jews of all ages and backgrounds who seek to repair our broken world. I have no doubt that were Heschel alive today, he would be a leader in the fight for justice, democracy, and religious pluralism in Israel, for a just solution to the occupation of the Palestinian people, for our responsible stewardship of the earth, and so much more.

"To be is more essential than to have. Though we deal with things, we live in deeds," Heschel wrote in our studied text, *The Earth Is the Lord's*. I underscored these sentences at age sixteen—saying that this represented the "feeling of youth today," in my penciled scrawl. The same sentiment could be written fifty-one years later. There is an agelessness in Heschel that speaks again and again to us, to anyone who is open to it—and anew for new generations.

As is stressed in chapter 4 of this book, Heschel taught that "the mitzvah is a key . . . to the gates of faith. . . . By living as Jews we may attain our faith as Jews." It is this teaching, to live our values as a pathway to God, in however we define it, that I believe was so resonant not only for me as a young student, but for so many young Jews today.

Harold Kasimow was my teacher decades past, and he is still my teacher. In reading this book, I learned new insights into Heschel. This study, like Heschel's teachings, is timeless and important.

Jo-Ann Mort

Abbreviations

GSM	*God in Search of Man*
IF	*Insecurity of Freedom*
K	*Kotzk*
MNA	*Man Is Not Alone*
MQG	*Man's Quest for God*
P	*Prophets*
PT	*Passion for Truth*
WM	*Who Is Man?*

1

Major Influences on Heschel's Thought

HASIDIC MASTERS HAD THE most profound influence on Heschel's theology, even as he was open to other significant influences. This was especially true of the Baal Shem Tov and the Kotzker Rebbe.

Heschel was born in Warsaw, Poland, in 1907. During the first twenty years of his life, like other East European Jews, Heschel immersed himself in the study of biblical rabbinic and mystical Jewish literature. The scholar Fritz Rothschild noted that "at the age of ten he was at home in the world of the Bible; he had acquired competence in the subtle dialectic of the Talmud and had also been introduced to the world of Jewish mysticism, the Kabbalah."[1]

Yet, unlike most Jews of his time and place, Heschel also delved deeply into secular studies. He relates how at the age of twenty he went "with great hunger to the University of Berlin to study philosophy."[2] He soon came to realize, however, the profound difference between his own views and those of his professors. Heschel

1. Rothschild, *Between God and Man*, 11.
2. Heschel, *Man's Quest for God*. Cited hereafter as *MQG*.

was not enamored with what he labeled the "Greek-German way of thinking" practiced by his professors at the University of Berlin.

While Heschel was a student in Berlin he became deeply involved in the study of the great medieval Jewish philosophers, and although he had the greatest respect for these scholars, his approach to Judaism and the conclusions he reached on essential issues contrast sharply with their views. Most of the Jewish philosophers in the Middle Ages were Sephardim, Jews who lived in Spain. Their weakness, according to Heschel, was that they neglected some of the essential features of Judaism, in their attempt to reconcile Judaism with the ideas of the great Greek and Muslim thinkers, fashionable at the time.[3]

Who, then, were the major spiritual forces which shaped Heschel's thought? For Heschel, the Bible was paramount. As he wrote in *God in Search of Man*, "The presence of God is found in many ways, but above all God is found in the words of the Bible."[4] Still, there can be no doubt that the Talmud, especially the ideas of Rabbi Akiva and Rabbi Ishmael, had a great influence too in shaping Heschel's thought. Yet neither the Bible nor the Talmud replaced the influence of the Hasidic masters on Heschel's approach to religion. For Heschel, the Baal Shem Tov and the Kotzker Rebbe were preeminent.

"Throughout my entire life the words of the Kotzker Rebbe burned within me," Heschel wrote.[5] But the Kotzker was not the only Hasid whose words burned in Heschel's heart. Heschel revered another rebbe, the Baal Shem Tov, founder of the Hasidic movement. He writes: "I must admit that during my entire life I struggled between being a Hasid of the way of the Baal Shem or the way of the Kotzker Rebbe. There are moments in my life—may God forgive me for my Chutzpah—when I think and feel like a Kotzker Hasid."[6]

3. Heschel, "Two Great Traditions," in *Earth Is the Lord's*, 23–38.

4. Heschel, *GSM*, 25.

5. Heschel, *Kotzk*, 7. This quotation is from the Yiddish original and all other quotations from this book are my translations. Cited hereafter as *K*.

6. Heschel, *K*, 10.

He continues: "I am the last one of a generation, perhaps the last Jew from Warsaw, whose soul lives in Mezibzh [the place where the Baal Shem spent the last twenty years of his life] and his mind in Kotzk."[7]

Rabbinic Judaism consisted at that time of the study of the Torah as an end in itself. Hasidism arose as a revolt against rabbinic Judaism, a reaction to the cold, formalistic, rigid teaching of the eighteenth century. As the great Jewish historian Simon Dubnow wrote, rabbinic Judaism at that time "failed to satisfy the religious cravings of the common man. The latter needed beliefs . . . making an appeal to the heart rather than the mind."[8] Even Heinrich Graetz, the great German Jewish historian, admitted that "Rabbinical Judaism, as known in Poland, offered no sort of religious comfort."[9] This, in spite of him having called Hasidism a "daughter of darkness."[10]

For Heschel, Hasidic Judaism answered a yearning to include three sacred entities—"God, Torah, and Israel."[11] The study of Torah took precedence over God, but Heschel insisted that the rabbis had forgotten that this study was but a path to God. "With many people, the attitude toward learning had become a kind of idolatry, depreciating the values of the heart," Heschel wrote. "Excessive *pilpul* (sophistry) had often dried up the inner wells and became the object of pretentious display of the intellect."[12]

For Heschel, many of the rabbis of this time fell prey to a doctrine that he labeled "religious behaviorism." He explains: "There are people who seem to believe that religious deeds can be performed in a spiritual wasteland, in the absence of the soul, with a heart hermetically sealed; that external action is the essential mode of worship; pedantry the same as piety, as if all that mattered

---

7. Heschel, *K*, 10.

8. Dubnow, *History of the Jews*, 1:221–22.

9. Graetz, *History of the Jews*, 5:385.

10. Graetz, *History of the Jews*, 5:385.

11. Abraham J. Heschel, "God, Torah and Israel," in Long and Handy, *Theology and Church*, 71.

12. Heschel, *Earth Is the Lord's*, 81.

is how men behaved in physical terms; as if religion were not concerned with the inner life."[13]

Is Heschel's "religious behaviorism" true to the spirit of the Talmudic sages to whom the Jewish spiritual elite had devoted all their lives? Heschel believed that this is a distortion of the spirit of rabbinic Judaism. Disciples do not always live up to the teaching of their masters. This distortion was not necessarily intentional; it occurred when the disciples stressed one idea over another, precisely what the rabbis did during the eighteenth century.

Indeed, the major struggle between Hasidism and rabbinic orthodoxy occurred because the rabbis became enamored with law (*halacha*) at the expense of inwardness (*aggadah*). Judaism is a religion of both *halacha* and *aggadah*, law and spirit. The Baal Shem Tov had no intention of doing away with *halacha*, but he was against its supremacy over *aggadah*.

Heschel agreed. He explains this most important polarity in Judaism:

> *Halacha* thinks in the category of quantity; *aggadah* is the category of quality. . . . *Halacha* speaks of the estimable and measurable dimensions of our deeds, informing us how much we must perform in order to fulfill our duty, about the size, capacity, or content of the doer and the deed. *Aggadah* deals with the immeasurable, inwards aspect of living, telling us how we must think and feel; how rather than how much we must do to fulfill our duty; the manner, not only the content, is important. To *halacha* the quantity decides; *aggadah*, for which quality is the ultimate standard, is not dazzled by either the number of the magnitude of good deeds but stresses the spirit, *kavanah*, dedication, purity.[14]

Perhaps Heschel was inspired by two other scholars, both of whom touch on this point. Bahya Ben Joseph Ibn Paquda, who wrote his classical work in Spain around 1080, *Duties of the Heart*, makes a similar point when he writes, "Strive therefore with all

13. Heschel, *MQG*, 53–54.
14. Heschel, *GSM*, 337–38.

your might that your deeds shall be pure, even though they be few, rather than many but not pure. For that which is small in quantity, but impure is little and useless."[15] The Talmud includes this same opinion: "Jerusalem was destroyed only because people insisted on the letter of the law—and did not go beyond it."[16]

The aim of Judaism is to create harmony between this polarity in the Jewish tradition. Certainly, the rabbis who created the Talmud placed great emphasis on *halacha*, but *aggadah* was also very precious to them. They said: "If you desire to know the One who spoke and the world came into existence, study *aggadah*, for through this study you will realize who spoke and the world came into being and will cleave to his ways."[17]

Heschel, more than any other Jewish theologian of our time, has shown us the great role of *aggadah* for the Talmudic mind. He argues that *halacha* without *aggadah* is taking the life element out of Judaism because "religion is born of fire of a flame, in which the dross of the mind and soul is melted away. Religion can only thrive on fire."[18]

For Heschel, this fire was brought to Judaism by the Baal Shem Tov. To the Baal Shem Tov, the person who devotes himself to the Talmud is not necessarily the person who is close to God. Heschel understands this when he writes: "One of the most important new ideas from the Baal Shem Tov is that a Jew can devote himself to Torah and nevertheless remain far from God, that devotion to Torah is actually nice and precious, but the essential remains: to be near to God. The Baal Shem Tov once saw a student who was immersed in learning, and he said about him: He is so immersed in learning that he forgets that there exists a God in the world."[19]

---

15. Ibn Paquda, *Duties of the Heart*, 2:65.

16. Quoted by Agus in *Vision and the Way*, 129.

17. Heschel, *Theology of Ancient Judaism*, 1:1. My translation from the Hebrew original.

18. Heschel, *GSM*, 317.

19. Heschel, *K*, 50–51.

The Baal Shem Tov's idea that the Torah may not be the best way to approach God, and in fact, there may even be times when Torah study is a hindrance, was certainly revolutionary for that time. Hasidic masters like Schneur Zalman of Liadi, the founder of Chabad (1747–1813), stressed that Torah and intellectual study was primary. This was also advocated by the Kotzker Rebbe, who said, "There are many paths to God . . . but there is only one way that is certain: to study Torah."[20]

For the Baal Shem Tov, studying the Torah without penetrating your soul did not lead you to God. How does one approach God? With concentration (*kavanah*), with joy (*simcha*), with ecstasy (*hitlachavut*), said the master. *Hitlachavut*, the "ecstatic devotion and clearing to God"[21] is a central idea in the Baal Shem Tov's teachings. Heschel explains: "The Baal Shem Tov and his students believe that you must worship God with *hitlachavut*, with fire. The essential is fire in the soul. . . . A true Hasid prays with *hitlahavut*, studies with *hitlahavut*, lives with *hitlahavut*.[22]

The Baal Shem was also unique in his age for his strong emphasis on joy or *simcha*. When he began to preach, the Jewish of Eastern Europe were in a state of mourning. Life was difficult. Dr. Jacob Agus describes the times as "a pious puritanical age, when the rabbis and the common folk sought to outdo each other in heaping up mountains or prohibitions . . . 'enlarging their phylacteries' in a thousand different ways."[23]

The teachings of the Jewish mystics, widely recognized during this time, did not help to alleviate the immense sadness that had descended upon the Jews of Eastern Europe. The teachings of the great Jewish mystic Isaac Luria were being spread by his disciple Hayim Vital throughout the entire Jewish world. This teaching contributed greatly to the mood of sadness. Lurianic Kabbalah

20. Heschel, *K*, 142.

21. Friedman, *Touchstone of Reality*, 151.

22. Heschel, *K*, 39.

23. Agus, *Evolution of Jewish Thought*, 338.

"demanded austere self-denial, torturous penance and mortification," as the scholar Shalom Spiegel phrased it.[24]

The Baal Shem, however, denounced sorrow and sadness as a path to God. He insisted, as Heschel noted, that "God is not only the creator of earth and heaven. He is also the one 'who created delight and joy. . . .' The fire of evil can be better fought with flames of ecstasy than through fasting and mortification."[25]

By reordering it, the Baal Shem transformed one of the basic principles of Judaism. Heschel explains:

> The essence of Judaism consists of three things—love of God, love of Torah and love of Israel. The order in which these three entities are mentioned is extremely important. All are agreed that love of God comes first, then comes love of Torah and finally love of Israel. This is the order listed in the Zohar, and the Kotzker Rebbe agrees with this order that love of Torah precedes the love of Israel. The Baal Shem, however, dissents: for him, love of Israel takes precedence over the love of Torah.[26]

The spiritual giants of Judaism throughout the ages have always agreed that God holds the central position. But they were not unaware of the danger that the Torah could replace God in order of importance. Therefore, they constantly emphasized that "God is greater than the Torah. He who devotes himself only to Torah and does not cultivate awe of God is regarded as a failure. . . . The study of Torah is worthless when not accompanied by awe and fear of heaven."[27]

If we settle the question of God transcending Torah and Israel, we still must ask which is more important—love of Torah or love of Israel. It is not unusual to find in rabbinic sources the idea that Israel is, in fact, more important than Torah. The prophet

24. Spiegel, *Hebrew Reborn*, 141.

25. Heschel, *Earth Is the Lord's*, 75–76.

26. Heschel, *K*, 52.

27. Abraham J. Heschel, "God, Torah and Israel," in Long and Handy, *Theology and Church*, 75.

Elijah advised Jewish saints that Israel is more important.[28] Rabbi Simon Bar Yochai, in whose name the Zohar was handed down, concurs with the prophet, since, in his view, the Torah was created for the sake of Israel and not vice versa.[29] Judaism has stressed repeatedly the special love that the Jew must have for Israel. There is nothing radical in Moses Hayyim Luzzatto's idea that "the Holy One, blessed be He, loves a man to the extent that the man loves Israel."[30] The Baal Shem's idea that love of Israel takes precedence over love of Torah is not strange to the Jewish tradition.

Still, it was a revolutionary doctrine for eighteenth century rabbinic Judaism. The rabbis of the day had little love or respect for the Jewish masses. The scholar Wolf Zeev Rabinowitsch noted that rabbinical scholars "treated the 'ignorant' masses with contempt, until the two classes came to be divided by an antagonism so deep that they ceased to understand each other's language."[31] And writing about the social conditions at the time of the rise of Hasidism, Harry Rabinowicz clams that "the scholars had as little in common with unlettered masses as the Polish nobles had with the peasantry. The scholars lived in a rarefied world of their own, a world of *Tannaim, Amoraim,* and *Geonim*."[32]

Yet the Baal Shem came with a radical message. Heschel interprets his work this way: "The Baal Shem came with a new stress: it is possible to be a learned man and a denier of everything, and it in fact happens that *Am ha'aretz* does things for which the world exists."[33]

Heschel explains the basic principle of the Baal Shem: "For him, it stands as a major principle that God loves everyone, a

28. Abraham J. Heschel, "God, Torah and Israel," in Long and Handy, *Theology and Church*, 84.

29. Idem

30. Luzzatto, *Mesillat Yesharim*, 362.

31. Rabinowitsch, *Lithuanian Hasidism*, 1.

32. Rabinowicz, *World of Hasidism*, 27. *Tannaim: mischniach* rabbinic sages; *Amoraim:* oral rabbinic scholars; *Geonim:* Babylonian era sages.

33. Heschel, *K*, 53–54; literal translation is the "people of the land," or the Jewish people.

principle which was later expressed by Aharon Karlener: I want ... to love the greatest Zaddik in Israel as God loves the greatest sinner in Israel."[34]

These ideas of the Baal Shem captured Heschel along with the hearts of East European Jewry: that what is most important is a good heart, a heart filled with love and compassion, and not a sharp mind; that one does not approach God with sadness but with joy and ecstasy.

But Heschel's mind was also pulled in another direction, toward the teaching of the Kotzker Rebbe. Heschel wrote that he was "struck like lightening," by this rabbi.[35] Who was this man who impacted Heschel when he was only nine years old, and who, according to Heschel, "remained a steady companion and challenge"?[36]

Heschel begins his exploration into the life of the Kotzker Rebbe with the following Midrash:

> "Rabbi Shimon said: When God was about to create Adam, the ministering angels split into contending groups. Some said, 'Let him be created!' while others cried, 'Let him not be created!'
>
> Mercy said, 'Let him be created for he will do merciful deeds.' Truth said, 'Let him not be created, for he will be false!' ... What did the Holy One, blessed be He, do? He took Truth and cast it into the ground."[37]

For the Kotzker Rebbe, the passion for truth was like a raging fire, making the Baal Shem seem like a peaceful saint by comparison. That's why this Midrash burned like fire into the entire being of the Kotzker. "He knows that the truth lies buried in the earth, but the truth lives in the grave. The truth wants to be resurrected, but men do not allow it."[38] The aim of the Kotzker was to raise

---

34. Heschel, *K*, 52.

35. Heschel, "Heschel's Last Words," 13. See also Heschel, *Passion for Truth*, xv. Cited hereafter as *PT*.

36. Heschel, "Heschel's Last Words," 13.

37. Heschel, *PT*, 12–13. See also Freedman and Simon, *Midrash Rabbah*, 1:58.

38. Heschel, *K*, 14.

truth from the earth, to bring it back to life, for there is nothing in life that should not be sacrificed for the sake of truth. The Baal Shem was not consumed with this intense passion for truth; he believed "that in this world goodness stands higher than truth. To hell with truth for a bit of compassion. There exists only one reality: Goodness. What is Good—is, and what is not good does not even have existence. Evil is . . . a delusion."[39]

The Kotzker Rebbe believed, however, that there can be no compassion without truth. As the years went by and the truth could not be revived from its grave, the Kotzker became harsher with his disciples and with the entire world. He came to realize that even though every soul has a longing to arrive at the truth, many lost this longing. But there is something even more tragic; not only has man lost his longing for truth, but he also no longer even cares that this longing is lost to him.[40] The Kotzker was tortured by this thought: "Why does man dance the devil's dance and does not allow the truth to emerge from the ground and be resurrected?"[41]

The Kotzker found himself in a world of falsehood. It was a world "sinking in the mud," a world in hell. Menachem-Mendl of Kotzk "spits on this profane world."[42] In this search for truth, the Hasid must strike out against his own nature and against society. To engage in the war against falsehood, he must separate himself from the world.[43]

Yet Heschel argues that the Kotzker is not preaching asceticism. "Kotsk, like other Hasidism, did not preach asceticism, or negate this-worldliness; he merely said that in order to get to the truth man often has to go against himself and society."[44]

Asceticism is not his goal, but from Heschel's own writing it appears that the spirit of asceticism is certainly present in his teaching. "Mendel considers the body to be the great enemy. . . .

39. Heschel, *K*, 14.

40. Heschel, *K*, 14.

41. Heschel, *K*, 609.

42. Heschel, *K*, 223.

43. Heschel, *K*, 227.

44. Heschel, *Encyclopedia Judaica*, 10:1223.

He feels certain that to give in to the body causes the destruction of the soul."[45]

The difference in the spirit of the teaching of the Baal Shem is striking: "The Baal Shem does not accept the old idea that the body and the soul are waging a battle. The body must be a partner in worshipping God. Therefore, we have to go along with the natural needs of the body."[46]

The contrast between the Baal Shem and the Kotzker appears to be so dramatic that it almost seems that they lived in two different worlds. Heschel captures most profoundly their contrasting spirits. "We can look at the world with wonder and see a world full of evil and ugliness. Isaiah heard: 'the whole earth is full of His glory' (Isaiah 6:3). Job saw: 'the earth is given into the hand of the wicked' (Job 9:23). The Baal Shem Tov feels like the seraphim in Isaiah, the Kotzker feels like Job. From the Baal Shem Tov came out a song, from the Kotzker Rebbe comes out an awesome scream."[47]

These two contrasting Hasidic masters each drew many disciples. One inspired them with love and compassion, the other with fear, with dread, and even despair. A close disciple of the Kotzker Rebbe tells us that his hair used to stand up in dread each time he encountered the rebbe.[48] "The Kotzker believed that the world could not be saved with faith and good deeds, the world lacks fear, dread. . . . He inspired fear and trembling because he himself lived in dread. . . . He wanted one to fear a lie like fire, and wanted people to live in dread for God. . . . The falsehood in the world is a sickness . . . it is wild meat that must be cut out."[49]

The Kotzker's entire being is tortured by this question. This problem is addressed to God. "How could God throw the truth into the earth? How could he bury the truth in order to create man?"[50]

45. Heschel, *K*, 24.

46. Heschel, *K*, 23.

47. Heschel, *K*, 27.

48. Heschel, *K*, 506.

49. Heschel, *K*, 506.

50. Heschel, *K*, 609.

The Kotzker is tormented by the world that God created. He realizes that there are no answers for the ultimate questions that torture man. These ultimate questions take possession of him. He lives in hell in his present life, for he realizes that man can never win a victory over God. "It is totally not destined and not possible for flesh and blood to understand God's answer for the deepest human questions. The secrets of God and the mind of man do not match."[51]

Is there any purpose in asking these terrifying questions when there are no answers? The Kotzker answers, yes. It is true that no answers can be gained by man, but he must persist in his search. Heschel explains: "The Kotzker Rebbe apparently believed that it is God's will that man should not give up; it is the task of man to storm the heavens."[52]

Heschel considered the Kotzker Rebbe one of the most revolutionary thinkers not only in the Hasidic world but in the entire Jewish world. I believe that the Kotzker Rebbe shares some unique ideas with another radical thinker in Judaism—Koheleth. Koheleth reached the same conclusion as the Kotzker Rebbe regarding the ultimate questions. Koheleth felt that no matter how long or how intensely a man searches, he won't find truth. He won't receive answers for the tormenting questions of life. "When I set myself to acquire wisdom and see all the activity taking place on the earth, I saw that though a man sleep neither by day nor by night he cannot discover the meaning of God's work which is done under the sun, for the sake of which a man may search hard, but he will not find it, and though a wise man may think he is about to learn it, he will be unable to find it."[53]

But Koheleth did not follow his own advice. On the contrary. His long life was devoted precisely to this search for truth. Like the Kotzker whom he preceded by two thousand years, Koheleth knew that the yearning for truth was inflicted by God himself. "He also puts eternity in men's hearts, except that they may not discover

51. Heschel, *K*, 600.

52. Heschel, *K*, 600.

53. *Koheleth* 8:16–17.

the work God has done from the beginning to end."[54] This is an essential passage of Koheleth's, where he comes close to proclaiming that something of God is implanted in each of us; therefore, our greatest desire must be to know God and his way in the world.

Finally, Koheleth arrives at the conclusion that although God had implanted in man a desire to know God, this desire could never be fulfilled. Since the search is painful, why bother? So, he advises his students to abandon the search. Meanwhile, the Kotzker, as we have already seen, believed that we must indeed persist in the search, no matter how great the pain, since this is God's will. The final radical conclusion of Koheleth is, "All is vanity and chasing of wind." He repeats this basic idea about twenty times throughout his writing.

The Kotzker Rebbe was certainly tortured by this problem. He asked the following questions: "Does human existence have any meaning? Do we fool ourselves when we think we have accomplished anything in this world?"[55] The Kotzker agrees with Koheleth, who says "we do fool ourselves when we think that we have accomplished anything. Life has no meaning." The Kotzker tells us: "What we do is spill water into barrels with holes. Our work has no meaning, life is absurd, our deeds are vanity of vanities."[56] But he disagrees with Koheleth's idea that no effort should be made. "We must act because that is the will of God,"[57] he stresses.

Heschel continues to probe into this idea of the Kotzker Rebbe. Here is his argument. The Kotzker agrees with Koheleth that although a man may struggle day and night, he cannot accomplish anything. Apparently, life has no meaning. But, for the Kotzker, one thing has a meaning—truth, and living truth means not to fool ourselves, not to convince ourselves that life has meaning. All we really do is pour water into pots with holes, and yes, we think that we have accomplished something. But then the possibility occurs to us that God, who is Truth, fools us, tells us a lie. Yet,

54. *Koheleth* 3:11.
55. Heschel, *K*, 614.
56. Heschel, *K*, 615.
57. Heschel, *K*, 615.

how could we accept that the truth is telling us a lie or that God is fooling the world? The Kotzker will not go so far. Truth cannot tell a lie and God will not fool the world. There is a purpose, but it is hidden from us. Just as the truth lies buried the reason for human existence lies buried.[58]

In Kotzk, where truth and the reason for human existence lie buried, there is no peace. There is only anxiety, fear, and dread. But what can one do? We must live with this terrifying problem. We must live in the chamber of hell. For that is the will of God. Heschel, at this point, suggests that perhaps this is the reason that the Kotzker Rebbe locked himself up in his room for the last twenty years of his life. "He who lives with problems must live alone."[59] Though, it has also occurred to me that the Kotzker's separation from the world was in fact a revolt against God. Just as God buried truth in the earth, the Kotzker buried himself in his room.

Living with the Baal Shem, who gave Heschel wings, and the Kotzker, who encircled him with chains, was not easy for Heschel.[60] Heschel immersed himself in the Baal Shem, who also gave warmth like the sun, and the Kotzker, who was cold like the moon. His struggles must have been intense, yet Heschel refused to deny either master. He realized that "honesty, authenticity, integrity, without love, may lead to the ruin of others, of oneself, or both. While love, fervor or exaltation alone may seduce us into living in a fools' paradise—a wise man's hell."[61]

Heschel once presented the thought of Rabbi Akiva and Rabbi Ishmael to his rabbinical students at the Jewish Theological Seminary, of which I was one. He challenged us to determine with which rabbi he was more in agreement. The question before us is even more challenging—is Heschel in greater affinity with the Baal Shem Tov or with the Kotzker Rebbe? The greatest influence on Heschel was the way of the Baal Shem. Still, the influence of the Kotzker persists.

58. Heschel, *K*, 616–17.

59. Heschel, *K*, 616–17.

60. Heschel, "Heschel's Last Words," 13.

61. Heschel, "Heschel's Last Words," 13.

The scholar Maurice Friedman responds to this idea with a poetic answer: "I suspect that the Besht [Baal Shem] was the mountain, the Kotzker the underground river. Both are present but in different ways. How can you compare them quantitatively?"[62] I agree with Dr. Friedman's statement that "both are present in different ways." In fact, Heschel's statement, "I am the most maladjusted person in society," shows his strong affinity with the Kotzker. Like the Kotzker, Heschel could not adjust to the falsehood in the world. Yet, in fact, during the last years of his life, Heschel left his study more and more frequently to speak out against the falsehood and corruption he experienced around him. The action of Heschel's shows his difference from the Kotzker most dramatically. The Kotzker abandoned society because he was in despair over man's nature and condition. He turned his energies to do battle with God. Heschel, in the spirit of the Besht, never gave up on man. His great battle is not with God, but with man. Heschel's response to falsehood is also radically different from that of the Kotzker. For the Kotzker, the opposite of falsehood is truth (*sheker* vs. *emet*). For Heschel, the opposite of *sheker* is *emunah*, faith.[63] Yet, I agree with Dr. Friedman's emphatic statement which suggests that, during the last years of life, Heschel was very much under the spell of the Kotzker.

Heschel did live his whole life under the influence of the Kotzker Rebbe, but there is a tragedy in the life of Heschel with which even the Kotzker did not have to deal. That is Auschwitz. Heschel wrote, "I am really a person who is in anguish. I cannot forget what I have seen and been through. Auschwitz and Hiroshima never leave my mind."[64] Yet despite the influence of the Kotzker and having lived through the horrors of the Second World War, Heschel, like the Baal Shem Tov, begins with love. *God in*

62. Dr. Friedman also called my attention to the fact that *Who Is Man?*, a late work of Heschel's, has "more of the absurd" than his earlier works and that his last large study was on the Kotzker.

63. Sanders, "Apostle to the Gentiles," 63.

64. Heschel in conversation with Patrick Granfield, *Theologians at Work*, 81.

Search of Man opens with the statement that religion declined in our time because it lacks the element of love. Religion has failed to stress love and compassion, its true nature. Like the Baal Shem, Heschel sees a solution to this problem by acknowledging the existence of a world full of wonder and miracles. Although he believes, together with the Kotzker, that "the world is sinking in mud,"[65] Heschel insist that there exists, nevertheless, a path to God. On this point, the Baal Shem and Heschel are close to the biblical view of the world. According to Heschel, mankind sinks in the mud not because there are no answers, as the Kotzker claimed, but because contemporary man has forgotten how to ask ultimate questions. In order to ask ultimate questions, we must awaken to the biblical view of the world.

65. Heschel, *K*, 29.

2

The Path to God through the World

Heschel promotes a radical notion. He believed that we were required to have a complete transformation in how we view the world around us. In order for modern man to comprehend the new view, he must part with the Greek philosophers who were his guides and immerse himself in the view of biblical man. For Heschel, the Greek philosophers epitomized paganism.

He explains in this interview with Ronald Beck, in a conversation about the Catholic Church. "We live in a world which is dominated by pagan thinking and pagan categories and pagan modes of expression and response. Unless there is a continuous wrestling with what underlies the Hebrew Bible, a way of looking at the world in existence in that Hebrew prophetic way, then by necessity the Church is affected by other categories and modes of thinking."[1]

Heschel's statement applies equally to modern Jewish thinking. Jews—and Christians—today are affected by "pagan modes of expression and response." Heschel is rediscovering a way that was once known to biblical men. Heschel is not claiming that he has

1. Heschel, "God of Judaism and the Christian Renewal," n. p.

discovered a new way to God. Rather, he is rediscovering a way that was once known to biblical man and has since been forgotten. How does the modern approach to the world differ from that of biblical man? According to Heschel: "There are three aspects of nature that command our attention: its power, its beauty, and its grandeur. Accordingly, there are three ways in which we may relate ourselves to the world—we may exploit it, we may enjoy it, we may accept it in awe."[2]

It's difficult to argue with Heschel's belief that many people in our modern era are dominated by the power aspect of nature, or that they exploit that power over nature. Indeed, this is more prescient than ever. Heschel writes: "Our age is one in which usefulness is thought to be the chief merit of nature; in which the attainment of power, the utilization of its resources is taken to be the chief purpose of man in God's creation."[3]

Unlike our contemporary world, biblical man was enchanted not by the power aspect of nature but by its grandeur. The world elicits a response of awe and wonder rather than a desire to exploit it and control it.

This goes to the heart of Heschel's philosophy. He believes that there can be no true religion without wonder. Wonder, in fact, is the fundamental attitude of the truly pious person. Certainly, Maurice Friedman is correct and perceptive when he calls Heschel "the philosopher of wonder,"[4] for Heschel himself states that "awareness of the divine begins with wonder."[5]

Heschel identifies biblical terms that are essential for understanding the biblical view of the world. The scholar Fritz Rothschild identifies these terms: "six terms that describe grandeur and man's reaction to it in three correlative pairs: the sublime and wonder, mystery and awe, the glory and faith."[6] Heschel, himself, defines the first pair of terms essential to his understanding of the realm of

2. Heschel, *GSM*, 33–34.

3. Heschel, *GSM*, 34.

4. Friedman, "Abraham Joshua Heschel: Philosopher," 12–14.

5. Heschel, *GSM*, 46.

6. Rothschild, *Between God and Man*, 11.

the ineffable or, as he sometimes calls it, the "holy dimension," as "sublime" and "wonder." He explains: "The sublime is that which we see and are unable to convey. It is the silent allusion of things to a meaning greater than themselves . . . It may be sensed in every grain of sand, in every drop of water. Every flower in the summer, every snowflake in the winter, may arouse in us the sense of wonder that is our response to the sublime."[7]

Heschel sees this nurturing of nature as something that makes us essentially human. He even states that if our eyes can no longer see the grandeur of nature, we can no longer sense the sublime, then we are no longer fully human. He writes: "The beginning of our happiness lies in the understanding that life without wonder is not worth living. What we lack is not a will to believe but the will to wonder."[8] Later, he is even more forceful, when he declares: "Man will not die for lack of information. It will perish for lack of appreciation. Unless there is appreciation there is no mankind. The great marvel of being alive is the ability to discover the mystery and wonder of everything. . . . Unless we learn how to revere, we will not know how to exist as human beings."[9]

Attaining wonder is of the highest order for Heschel. It is "the beginning of our happiness." It is not a state of nirvana; on the contrary, "endless wonder is endless tension."[10] There is a thread here between Heschel and Asian religions, which I will explore later in this book.

Mystery is also key to Heschel. When he describes the ineffable realm, he does not turn to the prophets or to Psalms, as is usual for him. He turns instead to Wisdom literature, beginning his examination of mystery by quoting from Koheleth:[11] "I said, I

---

7. Heschel, *GSM*, 39.

8. Heschel, *Man Is Not Alone*, 37. Cited hereafter as *MNA*.

9. Heschel, "God of Judaism and the Christian Renewal," n. p.

10. Heschel, *GSM*, 112.

11. I will usually refer to Koheleth, using the Hebrew word for the biblical book, but it is more familiarly known in the Greek as Ecclesiastes.

will be wise, it was far from me. That which is, is far off and deep, exceedingly deep. Who can find it out?"[12]

Heschel explains: "Ecclesiastes is not only saying that the world's wise are not wise enough, but something more radical. What is, is more than what you see: What is, is 'far off and deep, exceedingly deep.' Being is mysterious."[13]

Koheleth is no doubt unique among books of the Hebrew Bible, radically diverging on many essential ideas from the other books.[14]

Koheleth does not contend, however, that the idea "that the existence of the world is a mysterious fact."[15] There is more that is apparent than not. According to Heschel, there is nothing that does not hold a great secret for biblical man. "What stirred their souls was neither the hidden nor the apparent, but the hidden in the apparent; not the order but the mystery of the order that prevails in the universe."[16]

A pious person needs both the sense of the sublime and the sense of mystery to exist. Heschel writes, "The root of worship lies in the sense of the 'miracles that are daily with us.' There is neither worship nor ritual without a sense of mystery."[17]

For Heschel, biblical man does not respond to mystery with a sense of resignation, with fear, or terror, but with awe. "Awe . . . is the sense of wonder and humility inspired by the sublime or felt in the presence of mystery."[18] Just as there is no faith without wonder, Heschel argues that there is no faith without awe. He explains: "Awe precedes faith; it is at the root of faith. We must grow in awe

12. *Koheleth* 7:23–24.

13. Heschel, *GSM*, 54.

14. According to Scott, it is not possible to bring Ecclesiastes "into line with the tone and teaching of the rest of the Bible. It diverges too radically." Scott, *Proverbs-Ecclesiastes*, 191.

15. Heschel, *GSM*, 56.

16. Heschel, *GSM*, 56.

17. Heschel, *GSM*, 62.

18. Heschel, *GSM*, 62.

in order to reach faith. . . . Awe rather than faith is the cardinal attitude of the religious Jew."[19]

Having established mystery and awe as pre-eminent, Heschel turns to the third concept that he considers so crucial, namely the glory of God. He considers the ancient controversy between two dynamic concepts found in biblical literature, the transcendence and the immanence of God.

Some scholars argue that Judaism has suffered from an undue stress on God's transcendence, claiming that God's immanence has been completely neglected. For instance, in his classic work on rabbinic Judaism, George Foot Moore writes: "In the endeavor to exalt God uniquely above the world, Judaism, it is said, had in fact exiled him from the world in lonely majesty, thus sacrificing the immediacy of the religious relation. . . . In exaggerated forms of this theory . . . the God of Judaism is qualified as 'absolute' or 'transcendent.'"[20]

It is certainly true that historical Judaism has stressed the transcendence, the holiness of God, but it has equally stressed the immanence and the glory of God. In fact, Heschel emphasizes in all of his work that "Jewish thinking and living can only be adequately understood in terms of a dialectic pattern, containing opposite or contrasted properties."[21]

Indeed, we can find a dialectical pattern in biblical thought, in this phrase from the book of Isaiah: "Holy, holy, holy is the Lord of Hosts; the whole earth is full of His glory."[22] This verse clearly presents us with holiness—the transcendence of God—as well as with the glory and immanence of God. "The whole earth is full of His glory" has always been understood by Jews to mean the whole earth is full of God's presence, which was later called the Shechinah. One Jewish scholar, Joshua Abelson, ordained as a liberal rabbi in London, wrote as an introduction of his book, *The Immanence of God in Rabbinical Literature*, in 1913 that "Rabbinic

19. Heschel, *GSM*, 62.

20. Moore cites "Christian Writers on Judaism," 197–254, especially 226ff. Moore, *Judaism*, 1:423.

21. Moore, *Judaism*, 341.

22. Isaiah 6:3.

Judaism is often flouted for its weakness and insubstantiality, because of its insistence upon Transcendence to the utter neglect of Immanence. It is to demonstrate that Immanence has not been neglected by those teachers, that it is a considerable feature of their doctrines, that this book has been written."[23]

In a chapter on "Prophetic Philosophy, Professor Israel Efros also substantiates the dialectical pattern of Jewish thought proposed by Heschel.

> Two opposing concepts have always operated in Jewish philosophy. . . . These concepts, which we may call Holiness (*Kedushah*) and Glory (*Kavod*), never existed separately because then Hebraic thought would have been expired either in a deistic frost or in a pantheistic flame. They were always intermingled, and it was all a question of dominance and emphasis, holiness tries to lift the God-idea ever above the expanding corporeal universe, and Glory tends to bring the Creator ever nearer to man.[24]

These scholars clearly highlight the existence of God's glory or presence in Jewish thought. Heschel attempts to describe this glory in spite of the fact that he tells us that "we have no words to describe the Glory; we have no adequate way of knowing it."[25]

For Heschel, the book of Isaiah reveals this glory.

> In his great vision Isaiah perceives the voice of the seraphim even before he hears the voice of the Lord. What is it that the seraphim reveal? "Holy, holy, holy is the Lord of Hosts; the whole earth is full of His Glory." Holy, holy holy—indicate the transcendence and distance of God. The whole earth is full of his glory—the immanence or presence of God. The outwardness of the world communicates something of the indwelling greatness of God. The glory is neither an aesthetic nor a physical quality. It is sensed in grandeur, but it is more than grandeur. *It is a presence or the effulgence of a presence.*[26]

23. Abelson, *Immanence of God*.

24. Efros, *Ancient Jewish Philosophy*, 7.

25. Heschel, *GSM*, 84.

26. Heschel, *Who Is Man?*, 89. Hereafter cited as *WM*.

He continues: "Standing face to face with the world, we often sense a presence which surpasses our ability to comprehend. The world is too much for us. It is crammed with marvel. There is a glory, an aura, that lies about all beings, a spiritual setting of reality."[27]

Heschel believes that we have the possibility of experiencing this glory, that the presence of God is not closed to us; in fact, we experience it without realizing it. We are certainly capable of responding with wonder and radical amazement to the grandeur and the sublime. We are capable of responding with awe to the mystery, with faith to the glory. Why, then, do we fail? We fail because indifference dominates us. Heschel charts this: "This is the tragedy of every man: 'to dim all wonder by indifference.' Life is routine, and routine is resistance to the wonder. 'Replete is the world with a spiritual radiance, replete with sublime and marvelous secrets. But a small hand held against the eye hides it all,' said the Baal Shem. 'Just as a small coin held over the face can block out the sight of a mountain, so can the vanities of living block out the sight of the infinite light.'"[28]

Heschel does not find it easy to explain this holy dimension or the realm of the ineffable. For the modern reader, this concept is extremely difficult to comprehend. Yet, Heschel's message is very clear in a poetic sense: we must put down our hand from our eyes; we must open our ears if we want to experience the "infinite light."

Critically important for Heschel is that these truths take precedence over the survival of any particular religion or even the survival of religion itself. There is nothing specifically Jewish in this aspect of Heschel's first path to God's presence. For Heschel, the survival of humanity is the main issue. "The cardinal problem is not the survival of religion, but the survival of man," he states. "What is required is a continuous effort to overcome hardness of heart, callousness, and above all to inspire the world with the biblical image of man, not to forget that man without God is a torso, to

27. Heschel, *WM*, 90.
28. Heschel, *GSM*, 85.

prevent the dehumanization of man. For the opposite of human is not the animal. The opposite of the human is the demonic."[29]

Urgency is precisely Heschel's intention here. He believes that we have the power to create a demon: "Indeed, man's worship of power has resurrected the demon of power."[30] We live in a time "in which it is considered unreasonable to believe in the presence of the Divine,"[31] but quite reasonable to believe in the presence of the demonic. Man's resurrection of "the demon of power" is a difficult concept for Heschel, because "as a Jew, I recoil from the belief in the demonic."[32]

Heschel said, "as a Jew," but he could just as well have said, "as a human being." For Heschel, there is always hope for everyone to be capable of opening themselves to the holy dimension, that all of us possess the potentiality for sensing the ineffable: "[T]here is no man who is not shaken for an instant by the eternal."

Heschel faces a difficulty explaining his central concept because it is not rational. It is a mystical or contains a mystical element. He persists in describing this experience when he writes: "A sensitive person knows that the intrinsic, the most essential, is never expressed. . . . The stirring in our hearts when watching the star-studded sky is something no language can declare. What smites us with unquenchable amazement is not what we grasp and are able to convey but that which lies within our reach but beyond our grasp not the quantitative aspect of nature but something qualitative; not what is beyond our range in time and space but the true meaning, source, and end of being, on other words, the ineffable."[33]

According to Heschel, we are citizens in two realms.

> The tangible phenomena we scrutinize with our reason, the sacred and indemonstrable we overhear with the sense of the ineffable. The force that inspires readiness

29. Heschel, "What We Might Do Together," 135.
30. Heschel, "What We Might Do Together," 134.
31. Heschel, "What We Might Do Together," 133.
32. Heschel, "What We Might Do Together," 133.
33. Heschel, "What We Might Do Together," 134–35.

for self-sacrifice, the thoughts that breed humility within
and behind the mind, are not identical with the logi-
cian's craftmanship. The purity of which we never case
to dream, the untold things we insatiably love, the vision
of the good for which we either die or perish alive—no
reason can bound. It is the ineffable from which we draw
the taste of the sacred, the joy of the imperishable.[34]

Heschel believes that we cannot equate the meaningful with
the expressible, since that would ignore an entire realm of human
experience of which only the sense of the ineffable is aware. Yet
even though we cannot define or describe it, "it is given to us to
point to it."[35]

Heschel's biblical approach to God, through the realm of
the ineffable, forces us to see Judaism in particular, and religion
in general, in a new light. It is a biblical path. It has not been a
rabbinic path. The approach to God through the world, through
nature, was not emphasized by rabbinic Judaism. It was revived
by Hasidism, which of course was decisive for Heschel's thought.

For both the Baal Shem and Heschel, attachment to nature
and to beauty is not irreverent. As A. Shauli writes, "The Baal
Shem's attachment to nature is far removed from the warnings of
the rabbis in the Mishnah against interrupting one's study to say,
'How lovely that tree is' . . . . Sensuous beauty is but a spark and a
place reflection of the source of true beauty which is in the spirt."[36]

According to Heschel, it is problematic that we don't say au-
tomatically, "How lovely is that tree." The awareness of grandeur
and the sublime has all but disappeared from the contemporary
mind. Heschel's task in the first path is to teach the world how to
sense wonder and awe, how to see the holy in the everyday. "Sanc-
tification is not an unearthly concept. There is no dualism of the
earthly and the sublime. All things are sublime."[37]

34. Heschel, "What We Might Do Together," 139.
35. Heschel, "What We Might Do Together," 121.
36. Shauli, "Hasidic Legend and Aphorism," 229.
37. Heschel, *MNA*, 267.

To gaze at a lovely tree, for Heschel, is an act of love for God, since the tree is a work of God's. Heschel illustrates this point with this parable that was told by Rabbi Nachman of Bratzlav. It's the story of the homesick prince who experiences great joy when he realizes his father's presence in the form of a letter.[38] The prince misses his father so much, he can't stop mourning the loss—until he realizes that the letter was written by the hand of his father, and that, indeed, the letter represents the father's presence.

Influential Christian and Jewish theologians reacted to the path that Heschel lays out. In his review of *Man Is Not Alone*, which is devoted primarily to the first path, Reinhold Niebuhr, a great friend and colleague of Heschel's, writes: "This volume is so impressive because it is the work of a poet and mystic who has mastered the philosophical and scientific disciplines and who with consummate skill reveals the dimension of reality apprehended by religious faith."[39]

Jewish thinkers also did not fail to see the profound nature of Heschel's work. Maurice Friedman claimed that "Actually, *Man Is Not Alone* has as much power to speak to the uncommitted as any book that American Jewish thought has produced."[40]

Eugene Borowitz, an influential Reform rabbi and teacher, praises Heschel when he comments on Heschel's first path.

> Modern man has made himself unnatural by training himself not to be amazed, by working hard at not responding to the world in awe. That is the root affliction of an age anxious to the point of personal paralysis and moral incapacity. What men need most today is to recapture that radical amazement which is the most basic level of faith. They need to let themselves ask once again with full force and fervor: why is there anything at all? Why is it so wondrous, so unexpected?
>
> Why is it men can even ask and marvel? Here Heschel's felicity with images make its most impressive display. He is addressing an audience dulled by

38. Heschel, *GSM*, 99.

39. Niebuhr, "Masterly Analysis of Faith."

40. Friedman, "Abraham Joshua Heschel: Toward," 2.

the demythologization of nature and desensitized by sermons through science. Argument will not evoke awe, only another sort of technical, rational understanding. So, Heschel writes so as to illuminate, and like the great painters and photographers, he makes us see what we have seen a thousand times but never as truly as now. Had Heschel done no more than to remind me how the lens of faith brings a new depth of focus to the way one sees the world, he would have accomplished a major theological task. To have done so in an age which is so jaded to the amazement of existence that it had forgotten that nothing should be taken for granted can only be called healing.[41]

Even while agreeing with Borowitz that Heschel has accomplished a major theological task, we must be cautious and listen to Heschel. According to Heschel, his own first path is not sufficient. "The sense of wonder, awe and mystery is necessary but not sufficient to find the way from wonder to worship, from willingness to realization, from awe to action."[42]

He continues: "It is not a feeling for the mystery of living, or a sense of awe, wonder, or fear, which is the root of religion; but rather the question *what to do* with the feeling for the mystery of living, what to do with awe, wonder or fear."[43]

Next, we will examine how indeed "to live in a way that is compatible with the grandeur, the mystery, and the glory."[44]

41. Borowitz, "Abraham Joshua Heschel," 1515.

42. Heschel, *GSM*, 108.

43. Heschel, *GSM*, 112 and 162.

44. Heschel, *GSM*, 163.

3

The Path to God through Revelation

WHAT DO WE MEAN when we use the word "Bible"? What does it signify? Is the Bible one of the great treasures of Judaism because it contains "the historical religious experience of the Jewish people," or because it is one of the greatest masterpieces of world literature "ranked with the words of Shakespeare by literary critics"?[1] Or is the Bible the most precious written word the Jews possess because it is Torah *min ha-shamayim*, "Torah from heaven," which came into being "by way of prophecy or revelation"?[2]

Heschel believes that because the Bible came into being by way of revelation, it contains a divine element. That's why modern man can encounter the presence of God through the study of the Bible. As Heschel puts it: "The presence of God is found in many ways, but above all God is found in the words of the Bible."[3]

Heschel is not unique in his assertion that the Bible is the ideal path through which man can encounter God. Indeed, this is

1. Daiches, "Influence of the Bible," 1114.

2. Heschel, *GSM*, 167.

3. Heschel in conversation with Patrick Granfield, quoted by Granfield in his *Theologians at Work*, 77.

an integral part of Jewish tradition. Norman Lamm, a prominent Orthodox rabbi, writes: "It is in Torah that God is most immediately immanent and accessible, and the study of Torah is therefore not only a religious commandment per se, but the most exquisite and the most characteristically Jewish form of religious experience and communion."[4]

Professor Aharon Lichtenstein, discussing the character of biblical revelation, writes:

> Revelation is not only an objective datum or the process of its transmission, important as these may be. It is the occasion, exalting and humbling both, for a dialectical encounter with the living God. Revelation is not only a fixed text but in relation to man, an electrifying I-and-Thou experience.
>
> Moreover, this experience is not confined to the initial moment of divine giving and human taking of a specific message. It is repeated recurrently through genuine response to God's message which ushers us into His presence.[5]

Yet mere biblical study will not disclose God's presence. We must approach the Bible with our entire being. Here is a Hasidic story that exemplifies the importance of the Bible. Rabbi Moshe of Kobryn said: "When you utter a word before God, then enter into that word with every one of your limbs." One of his listeners asked: "How can a big human being possibly enter into a little word?" The Zaddik replied: "Anyone who thinks himself bigger than the Word is not the kind of person we are talking about."[6]

Malcolm Diamond, a Buber scholar, comments on this story: "By entering into the word with every one of his limbs, that is, by bringing the sum total of his life's experience to the reading of the Bible and holding himself open to the possibility of fresh response,

4. Norman Lamm, in Editors of *Commentary Magazine, Condition of Jewish Belief*, 125.

5. Aharon Lichtenstein, in Editors of *Commentary Magazine, Condition of Jewish Belief*, 133.

6. Buber, *Tales of the Hasidism*, 169.

the man of today may encounter the revelatory significance embodied in the texts."[7]

So, Abraham Heschel's real contribution to contemporary Judaism is not in his expounding that the Bible is a path of God, for many Jewish scholars have done—and continue to do—just that. Rather, Heschel's amazing contribution is first of all his original interpretation of prophecy or revelation, and second, the poetic manner of his writing. Because of Heschel, the Bible comes to life for both Jews and Christians. His unique literary style has such a tremendous impact on so many people.[8]

There is yet another reason why Heschel's contribution to Judaism is unprecedented. Other Jewish theologians who have examined the meaning of revelation have failed to tell us why we should believe in revelation. Heschel tells us. Painfully aware that the majority of people are not concerned with revelation, and mindful of the ever-increasing number of young Jewish and Christian seekers who deeply question the enduring problems of religious life, Heschel directs his attention to the truth of revelation, as well as to its meaning. He sets before himself a two-fold task—to present and interpret the meaning of revelation while also confronting us with its reality.

For Heschel, revelation is not a myth but a reality. The Bible is not only the word of man. It is also the word of God. Heschel's examination of revelation speaks directly to our modern world. Heschel delves into why, in the modern world, "the most serious problem is the absence of the problem."[9] Heschel's pivotal *God in Search of Man* examines this precise problem. From the first paragraph in the book, he examines the causes that led to the decline of religion, contending that we must not blame secular science or

---

7. Diamond, *Martin Buber*, 95.

8. The following articles discuss the power of Heschel's writing style: Friedman, "Abraham Joshua Heschel," and "Thought of Abraham Heschel"; Holtz, "Religion and the Arts"; Kaplan, "Form and Content," and "Language and Reality."

9. Heschel, *GSM*, 168.

anti-religious philosophy for this decline. The central cause lies within religion itself.

> "Religion declined not because it was refuted, but because it became irrelevant, dull, oppressive, insipid. When faith is completely replaced by creed, worship by discipline, love by habit; when the crisis of today is ignored because of the splendor of the past; when faith becomes an heirloom rather than a living fountain; when religion speaks only in the name of authority rather than with the voice of compassion—its message becomes meaningless."[10]

Heschel's words, while true, do not seem fully adequate. They overlook the fact that during the Middle Ages religion suffered from these same flaws, yet the mind of medieval man was dominated by religion. Today, modernity dominates us with science. Heschel realizes that there are good and sufficient reasons for the decline of religion from without as well as from within. He addresses himself, for instance, to the idea of revelation. "Resistance to revelation—religion—in our time came from two diametrically opposed conceptions of man: one maintained that man was too great to be in need of divine guidance, and the other maintained that man was too small to be worthy of divined guidance."[11]

Heschel's second reason for the decline of revelation—that man felt small and even insignificant when he compared himself with the cosmos—is not a very significant cause. However, Heschel's first argument, that man's self-sufficiency should be taken very seriously, deserves more attention.

The decline in the concept of revelation can be traced back to the Age of Reason from 1687 to 1790, from Isaac Newton's *Principia* to Immanuel Kant's *Critique of Pure Reason*.[12] During this time, reason gained in ascendancy, becoming the main guide to truth. This period was a rationalistic-scientific age where the truth of religion suffered its greatest blows. It was a naturalistic outlook[13]

10. Heschel, *GSM*, 3.

11. Heschel, *GSM*, 169.

12. Beck, *Eighteenth Century Philosophy*, 1.

13. Stace, *Religion and the Modern Mind*, 159. Here Stace uses the words

on the world, generally associated with materialism and positivism, best exemplified in the philosophical works of David Hume (1711–76).

Walter T. Stace writes that Hume "was the master builder of the naturalistic view of the world—so far as its expression in the abstract form of philosophy is concerned. . . . His thought is the very quintessence of the dominant philosophical trends of the modern world."[14] But Hume and his followers were not the only existing views of that time. There remained some saints and mystics. For instance, William Law (1686–1761), a famous mystic, declared that "religion need not submit itself to any test of reason."[15]

And, obviously, organized religion did not end when the age of reason reigned. One system of truth has never been able to dominate every other system in a given age. Nevertheless, certain time periods are dominated by principal trends of religious and philosophical thought. As Dr. Randall noted, "It is possible to find in the eighteenth century a fairly definite, coherent, and systematically organized body of beliefs and ideals, to which the great majority of the intellectual classes gave assent."[16]

The Romantic protest against the Age of Reason was already beginning before the end of the eighteenth century. There are various streams in Romanticism, but the movement was largely united in its attack on reason. The Romanticists felt that the rationalist-scientific picture of man as a "coldly calculating thinking machine" was most degrading. Instead, they stressed the emotional, the intuitional, and the mystical side of man. Thus, the rise of the Romantic spirit enabled the religious view of man and the world to assert itself once again. Although the spirit of Romanticism has had a profound effect on subsequent generations, including our own, still the dominant worldview today remains rationalistic and scientific, a perspective originating in the Age of the Enlightenment. Heschel described this when he wrote: "It is characteristic

"scientific" and "naturalistic" synonymously.

14. Stace, *Religion and the Modern Mind*, 174.

15. Randall, *Making of the Modern Mind*, 298.

16. Randall, *Making of the Modern Mind*, 389.

of the inner situation of contemporary man that the plausible way to identify himself is to see himself in the image of a machine. . . . Man is simply 'a machine into which we put what we call food and produce what we call thought.' The definition itself goes back to the eighteenth century. Never before, however, has it been so widely accepted as plausible."[17]

Heschel admits that this is the condition of our age. As the rationalistic-scientific worldview becomes more sophisticated, it also becomes more deeply materialistic. Transcendence diminishes considerably when a materialistic outlook that enhances man's sense of immediacy becomes preeminent.

Though he wrote in 1926, Dr. Randall's arguments are prescient today. He agrees that we are in an atmosphere of immediacy and that, "in a sense, all our modern philosophies, from socialism to the worship of business success, are but elaborations of the means for eating, drinking, and being merry in the most satisfactory way. Whether we acknowledge it or not, the modern age has been in fundamental agreement with the Omar . . . who taught this: Let us eat, drink, and be merry, for tomorrow we die."[18]

Heschel describes contemporary man similarly when he writes: "Needs are looked upon today as if they were holy, as if they contained the quintessence of eternity. Needs are our gods, and we toil and spare no effort to gratify them. Suppression of a desire is considered a sacrilege that must inevitably avenge itself in the form of some mental disorder."[19] It is truly extraordinary that decades later, these words of Heschel ring true. He anticipated our contemporary world beyond his wildest expectations. Neither Randall nor Heschel could have imagined the emergence of social media and its impact on our life, where everything can become immediate or superficial.

Indeed, in writing this book before this new edition, it must be said that I, too, could not have anticipated the prescience of Heschel's thinking.

17. Heschel, *WM*, 23–24.

18. Randall, *Making of the Modern Mind*, 594–95.

19. Heschel, *MNA*, 186.

Heschel concludes his point with a statement that eerily defines our world today—if taken metaphorically, considering that it first appeared in the book *God in Search of Man* in 1955. "More people die in the epidemics of needs than in the epidemics of disease," he wrote.[20]

"There can be little doubt that our age is more intensely involved in the search for sensual satisfactions than at any other time in history. Yet, there is general unhappiness around us. Insecurity, hunger, boredom, feelings of futility and of absurdity are rampant everywhere. Wars and revolutions, crime, suicide, mental disease, and other evidences of deep-seated social maladies flourish apace, some of them on a scale hitherto unknown."[21]

Will Herberg, the respected theologian and sociologist of religion, put it even more starkly. "Today . . . man has brought himself and his universe to the brink of destruction. The world for twentieth-century man is going out with a 'whimper and a bang.' . . . Horrors which yesterday we all believed had been banished once and for all from human society—slavery and despotism, vile superstition, famine and torture, persecution for opinion—have come back in the most virulent form. . . . Today the very survival of mankind has become problematical."[22] While we did make it through the twentieth century, albeit with many of the ills that Herberg lays out here, we find ourselves today in the twenty-first century living amid a list of these same horrors, and perhaps more.

It would appear, then, that the major cause for the decline of religion in general, and revelation in particular, does not lie with religion itself, but with the rationalistic-scientific view of the Age of Reason. When the exponents of reason went so far as to proclaim reason to be the only guide to truth, they in effect were saying that there was no longer any mystery that the human mind could not penetrate. "Whatever there is to know, that we shall

---

20. Heschel, *MNA*, 182.

21. Sorokin, *Crisis of Our Age*, 131.

22. Herberg, *Judaism and Modern Man*, 3, 5.

know someday."[23] When reason became the be-all and the end-all, revelation became unnecessary.

Dr. Randall describes the view of religion by eighteenth-century rationalists: "All of them agreed that religion is not an instinctive need and activity of the human soul, but essentially a science like physics, that is, a system of rational propositions given from without and to be tested as any other propositions are tested, by the evidence of the human reason."[24]

Randall points out that religion during the Age of Enlightenment became "merely a philosophical system appealing to the cool and deliberate reason of the man of common sense, and the inner experience of the presence of the divine, the immediate vision of God's living reality, was condemned as unwholesome 'enthusiasms'—the worst sin during the Age of Reason."[25]

Eighteenth-century thinkers attempted a harmonization between reason and revelation by making revelation subject to the laws of reason. In this type of reconciliation, faith of course faded into the background. Heschel notes: "If science and religion are intrinsically identical, one of them must be superfluous. In such reconciliation religion is little more than bad science and naïve morality."[26]

This opened the road to atheism. Reason had overthrown not only biblical revelation, but the religion of reason itself. "In 1798, a Deist started to address the Institute on his religious beliefs: there was a cry of anger from the assembled intellectuals, and one exclaimed, 'I swear there is no God, and I demand that his name be not pronounced in this place!'"[27]

The conclusion that there is no God still dominates the modern intellectual Western mind. Dr. Randall's assertion that reason is today in disrepute is only partially true.[28] Even today, despite the

23. Heschel, *GSM*, 34.

24. Randall, *Making of the Modern Mind*, 287.

25. Randall, *Making of the Modern Mind*, 290.

26. Heschel, *GSM*, 13.

27. Randall, *Making of the Modern Mind*, 304.

28. Randall, *Making of the Modern Mind*, 397.

nineteenth-century reaction to the Age of Reason and the attack on reason by some existentialists, the octopus of the rationalistic-scientific worldview has remained dominant.

Observations made by Stace back in 1952 are still relevant today. "The scientific view is in some sense the typical or dominant view of the modern world. It is what is characteristic of the modern mind, what marks it off from all other periods of history. . . . The twentieth century has witnessed . . . the strong resurgence of the scientific view of the world. We are now once more in its grip. . . . The scientific view appears to be the dominating and overpowering intellectual force of the present day."[29]

Peter Berger, the prominent sociologist of religion, in agreement with this view writes, "Whatever the situation may have been in the past, today the supernatural as a meaningful reality is absent or remote from the horizons of everyday life of large numbers, very probably of the majority, of people in modern societies, who seem to manage to get along without it quite well."[30]

Good evidence (still likely the case today) comes from Dr. McClelland, a behavioral scientist and a committed Quaker, when he writes, "I can hardly think of a psychologist of my generation who would admit publicly or privately to a religious commitment of any kind."[31]

Heschel rails against this worldview to argue for the reality of revelation. He does not disparage reason or science, but rather contends that reason and science on the one hand, and revelation on the other, work on different levels. They deal with different issues.[32] This thesis is essential to Heschel's theological structure. It is worth quoting at great length.

---

29. Stace, *Religion and the Modern Mind*, 159.

30. Berger, *Rumor of Angels*, 5. For a dissenting view which contends that the religious situation has hardly changed in the last six thousand years, see Greeley, *Unsecular Man*. For a resurgence of fundamentalism, see Quebedeux, *Young Evangelicals*.

31. McClelland, *Roots of Consciousness*, 119.

32. Here Heschel uses reason and science as synonyms since, in our age, "reason has often been identified with scientism." *GSM*, 19.

The Bible and science do not deal with the same problem. The Bible points to a way of understanding the world form the point of view of God. It does not deal with *being as being* but with *being as creation*. Its concern is not with ontology or metaphysics but with history and *meta-history*; its concern is with time rather than space.

Science proceeds by way of equations; the Bible refers to the unique and unprecedented. The end of science is to explore the facts and processes of nature; the end of religion is to understand nature in relation to the will of God. The intention of scientific thinking is to answer man's questions and to satisfy his need for knowledge. The ultimate intention of religious thinking is to answer a question which is not man's, and to satisfy God's need for man.

Science deals with relations among things within the universe, but man is endowed with the concern of the spirit, and spirit deals with the relations between the universe and God. Science seeks the truth about the universe; the spirit seeks the truth that is greater than the universe. Reason's goal is the exploration and verification of objective relations; religion's goal is the exploration and verification of ultimate personal relations.[33]

Heschel began to formulate his views on the role of reason and revelation early in his career, while he was immersed in the study of medieval Jewish philosophers. In his article "Reason and Revelation in Saadia's Philosophy," Heschel criticizes Saadia for the way in which he attempted to reconcile the two. He concludes this brilliant study by writing:

Religious faith precedes and transcends knowledge. It is an ultimate force in man, lying deeper than the stratum of reason and its nature cannot be defined in abstract, static terms. It is a sense of the transcendent, a dynamic quality, the ability to envision the invisible, to be stirred by what lies beyond the reach of reason or perception. It is a manifestation of man's position on the verge of God. Unlike knowledge, which is a quiet possession of

33. Heschel, *GSM*, 16–19.

the intellect, faith is an overwhelming force that enable's man to perceive the reality of the transcendent.[34]

Critics of Heschel point out that Heschel diverged from what his critics consider "the rationalist tradition in Jewish theology" because "unlike the majority of his predecessors, Heschel does not believe that reason can furnish us with the clue to ultimate reality."[35]

According to Heschel, reason cannot penetrate ultimate truth. But he argues that this was always the view of Judaism. "For all the appreciation of reason and our thankfulness for it, man's intelligence was never regarded in Jewish tradition as being self-sufficient. 'Trust in the Lord with all thy heart, and do not rely on thine own understanding.' (Proverbs 3:5)."[36]

Heschel even brings in Maimonides, the idol of the rationalists, to show that even Maimonides did not fail to point out the limitations of reason. "I say that there is a limit to human reason and as long as the soul resides within the body, it cannot grasp what is above nature, for nothing that is immersed in nature can see above it. Reason is limited to the sphere of nature and it is unable to understand that which is above its limits."[37]

Yet, it would be erroneous to conclude with regard to the role of reason in religion that Heschel agrees with the entire Jewish tradition. A study of the great thinkers of medieval Judaism reveals that Petuchowski is correct—Heschel does break with the medieval Jewish philosophers. He does not believe, as they did, that the existence of God can be discovered by means of rational demonstration. This idea was stressed not only by Maimonides and the more rationalistic thinker Gersonides (1288–1344), but it was even expressed by the pietistic Bahya ibn Paquda. For Bahya ibn Paquda, it is a duty to arrive at an understanding of the main principles of Judaism through reason itself. He believes that only

34. Heschel, "Reason and Revelation," 408.

35. Petuchowski, "Faith as the Leap of Action," 390.

36. Heschel, *GSM*, 19.

37. Heschel, *GSM*, 233.

then will a person truly worship God. Bahya writes: "The philosopher spoke the truth when he said: 'Only the prophet, by reason of his natural endowment or the distinguished philosopher through the wisdom he has acquired, is able to worship the First Cause. But all the rest worship someone else, since they cannot conceive of any being that is not composite.'"[38]

Bahya teaches that the person who attains to the highest category of belief is he who "knows how to adduce proofs of His existence and has arrived at a knowledge of the truth of His Unity by the method of rational investigation and by arguments that are right and reasonable."[39]

Contrasting with these major figures, Heschel's statement that "reason may be perverse," clearly demonstrates that his approach to religion diverges radically from the medieval Jewish philosophers. Nevertheless, the charge of "irrationalism" leveled against Heschel by Petuchowski is without merit. Petuchowski is simply wrong about Heschel when he writes that "There is danger in wallowing in the irrational. Moods are in need of the corrective of Reason and Judaism in the 20th century . . . cannot survive if it bypasses and permits itself to be bypassed by, the constant development of cognitive thought."[40] Indeed, twenty-first-century Judaism has proven not only Heschel right, but Petuchowski wrong.

Why, then, have a number of well-known Jewish scholars held that Heschel's interpretation of Judaism is not in keeping with Jewish tradition? Perhaps because Heschel's thought is in conflict with the rationalistic thought of Moses Maimonides. Heschel and Maimonides differ radically on God and revelation, which we will soon see. But this doesn't mean that Heschel's though is un-Jewish. Rather, as has been cogently argued, in his attempt to reconcile the Bible with philosophy and reason with revelation, Maimonides

---

38. Ibn Paquda, *Duties of the Heart*, 1:65. Note: for a study of rationalism in medieval Jewish thought, the following works are valuable: Guttman, *Philosophies of Judaism*; also, Husik, *History of Mediaeval Jewish Philosophy*; and Sarachek, *Faith and Reason*.

39. Ibn Paquda, *Duties of the Heart*, 65.

40. Petuchowski, "Faith as the Leap of Action," 397.

relied too heavily on the philosophy of Aristotle, failing to realize that his thought was not in accord with that of the Bible. Dr. Husik finds it surprising that the great "Sage of Fostat" could not escape Aristotle's influence, even when Aristotle's ideas contrasted with those of the Bible. For Aristotle, "intellectual contemplation is the highest good of man."[41] Judaism, for Husik, must consider the spiritual and emotional sides of man. The life of the intellect, solely, cannot be reconciled with the Hebrew Bible, for there is "no stress laid upon knowledge and theoretical speculation as such. The wisdom and the wise man of the book of Proverbs no more mean the theoretical philosopher than the fool and the scorner in the same book denote the one ignorant in theoretical speculation."[42]

So, it appears that Heschel is not "irrational" but wholly in accord with biblical thought when he insists that "religion is not within but beyond the limit of mere reason."[43] Heschel's contention that "revelation is a problem that eludes scientific inquiry"[44] certainly doesn't deserve to be labeled irrational. Rather, Heschel argues that the use of reason is essential for the religious life. "The employment of reason is indispensable to the understanding and worship of God, and religion withers without it,"[45] he says. He continues: "The insights of faith are general, vague, and stand in need of conceptualization in order to be communicated to the mind, integrated and brought to consistency. Without reason faith becomes blind, without reason we would not know how to apply the insights of faith to the concrete issues of living. The worship of reason is arrogance and betrays a lack of intelligence. The rejection of reason is cowardice and betrays a lack of faith."[46]

Heschel believes that the religious man (or what he also considers the whole human being) must not worship or reject reason. Rather, he must use it well, while he continues to have

41. Husik, *History of Mediaeval Jewish Philosophy*, 299.

42. Husik, *History of Mediaeval Jewish Philosophy*, 300.

43. Heschel, *GSM*, 20.

44. Heschel, *GSM*, 220.

45. Heschel, *GSM*, 20.

46. Heschel, *GSM*, 20.

faith. Heschel's position actually opens the way for the inclusion of revelation as a potent source for the knowledge of God.

Yet, importantly, in attempting to prove the authenticity of revelation, Heschel shows that reason and science are not obstacles to the validity of revelation. But Heschel goes a further step, since he wants to make revelation a reality. He attempts to prove the reliability of the prophets. Heschel's groundbreaking study of the prophets in fact appeals even more strongly to our reason in order to prove the authenticity of revelation.

He writes: "It is only through our sense of the ineffable that we may intuit the mystery of revelation. . . Revelation is a mystery for which reason has no concepts."[47] This statement seems to preclude the possibility of proving the validity of revelation through the use of reason. Heschel makes a strong point here by arguing that if reason is not able to intuit certainty with regard to religious revelation, at least it can point out that there are no rational grounds for denying revelation. In order to prove his point, he raises critical questions: "Are the prophets reliable? Is their testimony trustworthy?"[48]

For Heschel, there are only three ways to look at the prophets. "They told the truth, deliberately invented a tale, or were victims of an illusion. In other words, revelation is either a fact or the product of insanity, self-delusion, or a pedagogical invention the product of a mental confusion, or wishful thinking, or a sub-conscious activity."[49]

Heschel goes on to argue intensely for his first option, rejecting the other two ways of thinking about the prophets.[50] Here are his salient arguments against the second possibility. "Is it conceivable that men . . . who condemned the lie as a fundamental evil should have lived by a lie? . . . and it would be most fantastic to assume that, generation after generation, men of highest passion for

47. Heschel, *GSM*, 189.

48. Heschel, *GSM*, 189.

49. Heschel, *GSM*, 223.

50. Especially in *GSM*, chapter 24, and in *Prophets*, chapters 23 and 24. Cited hereafter as *P*.

truth, of deepest contempt for sham, all schemed and conspired to deceive the people of Israel."[51]

As for the third possibility, that the prophets were insane, Heschel writes: "The manner in which the prophets dealt with the issues of their own time and the fact that the solutions they propounded seem to be relevant for all times have compelled people in every generation to repeat a commonplace: the prophets were among the wisest of all men. Their message being ages ahead of human thinking, it would be hard to believe in the normalcy of our minds if we questioned theirs."[52]

Responding to Heschel's arguments that the prophets were not insane, Roderick Hindery comments: "To prove that the prophets were sane or useful social servants is not yet to prove that their world view was not illusory."[53] Heschel argues back that the prophets were not "victims of illusion,"[54] devoting a special section in *God in Search of Man* to this argument. Heschel asserts that the prophet, unlike the mystic, did not crave "communion with God." Rather, "revelation occurred against the will of the prophet." Heschel then asks, "Is not *the experience of resistance to the experience* a mark of truthfulness, authenticity, or is this, too, a part of self-deception?"[55] Heschel does not prove that the prophetic worldview was not in fact illusory.

Yet, we must remember Heschel's basic assumptions and intentions in dealing with the prophets. He insists that there are no empirical criteria by which we can absolutely prove once and for all that the prophetic worldview was not illusory. We cannot prove the validity of revelation. But at the same time, there are no scientific grounds that show this prophetic worldview to be false.[56] "The goal of our 'examination' of the prophets was not to furnish the

51. Heschel, *P.*

52. Heschel, *P*, 223.

53. A comment made on my PhD thesis.

54. Heschel, *GSM*, 224–27.

55. Heschel, *GSM*, 224 (emphasis added).

56. Heschel, *GSM*, 232.

prophets with a letter of recommendation," he posits, "but rather to point to the difficulty of an outright rejection of their claim."[57]

Heschel explains:

> The mark of authenticity of the divine character of revelation was not in outward signs, visible or sonorous; revelation did not hinge upon a particular sense-perception, upon hearing a voice or seeing a light. A thunder out of a blue sky, a voice coming from nowhere, an effect without a visible cause, would not have been enough to identify a perception as a divine communication. Immense chunks of natural reality, showers of light thrust upon the mind, would, even if they were not phantasmagorial, only manifest a force of nature, not God.
>
> This, it seems, was the mark of authenticity: the fact that prophetic revelation was not merely an act of experience but an act of *being experienced*, of being exposed to, called upon, overwhelmed and taken over by Him who seeks out those whom He sends to mankind. It is not God who is an experience of man; it is man who is an experience of God.[58]

Heschel's aim—to show that rational analysis does not disprove the reality of revelation—agrees with Judah Halevi, who argues that revelation is beyond the limits of reason. Just as it is not possible to prove the existence of God by rational analysis, in the same way it is not possible to prove the truth of prophecy.

Perhaps, more obvious to the contemporary mind is this comparison of Heschel's: "There are no proofs for demonstrating the beauty of music to a man who is both deaf and insensitive, and there are no proofs for the veracity of the prophet's claim to a man who is spiritually deaf and without faith and wisdom."[59] We must be open to receiving a demonstration of beauty in art, just as we must be open to experiencing faith and wisdom.

Of course, it can be argued that some of Heschel's contentions about the prophets are not convincing. This can jolt our modern

57. Heschel, *GSM*, 234.

58. Heschel, *GSM*, 229–30.

59. Heschel, *GSM*, 223.

minds, when he writes: "In calling the prophets to stand before the bar of our critical judgment, we are like dwarfs undertaking to measure the heights of giants."[60] Yet, Heschel's arguments for the validity of revelation, when taken as a whole, are subtly convincing. They may renew interest in the Bible itself, especially in a modern world in need of a way to sustain itself in the threat of global warming and other massive forms of extinction that require a look inward.

Let's examine Heschel's understanding of the meaning of revelation, a subject to which Talmudic, medieval, and modern Jewish theologians have devoted much mental energy, and a subject to which Heschel comes with a unique approach, offering a great contribution. First, here is a brief example of the classic views in the Jewish concept of revelation.

The normative idea of revelation, formulated by rabbinic Judaism and still held by Modern Orthodox thinkers, is presented in the Jewish confession of faith. "I believe with perfect faith that the whole Torah, now in our possession, is the same that was given to Moses our teacher, peace be unto him."[61]

There is a *Baraitha* from the Talmud that illustrates the implication of this statement.

> Because he hath despised the word of the Lord—this refers to him who maintains that the Torah is not from Heaven. And even if he asserts that the whole Torah is from heaven, excepting a particular verse, which, he maintains, was not uttered by God but by Moses himself, he is included in "because he hath despised the word of the Lord." And even if he admits that the whole Torah is from heaven, excepting a single point, a particular ad majus deduction or a certain *gezerah shawah*—he is still included in *"because he hath despised the word of the Lord."*[62]

The rabbis expanded on the idea that only Torah, in the narrow sense—the five books of Moses or the entire Hebrew

---

60. Heschel, *GSM*, 222.

61. Hertz, *Authorized Daily Prayer Book*, 253.

62. Sanhedrin 99a.

Bible—was received by Moses. They believed that the Torah was represented in the broadest sense, that the entire Jewish tradition, was revealed by God to Moses. They said: "When God revealed Himself at Sinai to give the Torah to Israel, he communicated it to Moses in order: Bible, Mishnah, Talmud, and Haggadah, as it says, *And God spoke all these words* (Ex. XX.1). Even the question a pupil asks his teacher God told Moses at that time."[63]

While the rabbis did make a distinction about whether the manner through which the message of God was communicated, ultimately, all of it is the true word of God, since all of it was revealed to Moses. Rabbi Louis Jacobs, a British theologian, made this point: "The whole body of Torah as we have it today in Bible, Talmud and Midrash is thought of as divine truth conveyed to men, partly through divine dictation (the Pentateuch), partly through varying degrees of divine inspiration (the rest of the Bible), partly through divine guidance (the teachings of the rabbis) and, because divine, infallible."[64]

Certainly, the great medieval Jewish philosophers and biblical commentators accepted this classical formulation of revelation. Moses Maimonides presents his view of revelation in his eighth principle of faith.

> That the Torah has been revealed from heaven. This implies our belief that the whole of the Torah found in our hands this day is the Torah that was handed down by Moses and that it is all of divine origin. . . . In handing down the Torah, Moses was like a scribe writing from dictation the whole of it, its chronicles, its narrative, and its precepts. It is in this sense that he is termed *mehokek* [copyist]. And there is no difference between verses like "And the sons of Ham were Cush and Mizraim, Phut and Canaan," and verses like "I am the Lord thy God" and "Hear, O Israel." They are all equally of divine origin and all belong to the "Law of God which is perfect," pure, holy, and true.[65]

63. Freedman and Simon, *Midrash Rabbah*, 3:536.

64. Jacobs, "Liberal Supernaturalism," 112.

65. Quoted by Jacobs, *We Have Reason to Believe*, 67.

Even Moses Nachmanides (1195–1270), who leaned toward the Jewish mystical tradition and sharply criticized many of the rationalistic ideas of Maimonides, essentially agrees with this statement of Maimonides. He writes in his classical commentary on Genesis: "Moses our teacher wrote this book of Genesis together with the whole Torah from the mouth of the Holy One, blessed be He."[66] Nachmanides also introduces the idea already found in the Talmud and Midrash that the Torah "preceded the creation of the world, and needless to say, it preceded the birth of Moses our teacher. . . . Thus Moses was like a scribe who copies from an ancient book."[67] This view—that the Torah was created two thousand years before the creation of the world, generally held by medieval Jewish scholars[68]—of course also precludes the possibility of any human element in the event of revelation of God's word. In this respect, both Maimonides and Nachmanides are excellent representatives of the recognized medieval Jewish view of revelation. The only major exception in this period is Abraham Ibn Ezra (1092–1167), who vaguely suggested that certain passages in the Torah were not in fact written by Moses.

Modern Orthodox Jewish thinkers are substantially in agreement with these rabbinic and medieval views of the Torah. Rabbi M. D. Tendler, my own teacher of Talmud at Yeshiva University, offers this accepted Modern Orthodox view when he writes:

> It is the foundation of our faith that God spoke unto Moses as a teacher instructs his pupil. . . . This prophecy, the Torah, was received by Moses accompanied by the necessary explanatory details. The actual words and sentence structure of this divine revelation are recorded in the Pentateuch—the five books of Moses.
>
> There is yet another record of divine revelation—the oral tradition, comprising the explanatory notes and details of the biblical ordinances recorded in the Talmud along with the later man-made rabbinic edicts. Thus the Pentateuch and the oral tradition are of equal authority,

66. Nachmanides, *Commentary on the Torah: Genesis*, 7.

67. Nachmanides, *Commentary on the Torah: Genesis*, 8.

68. Golomb, *Judah Ben Solomon Campanton*, 35.

are equally obligatory on all Jews as the direct instruc-
tions of God to his nation, Israel.[69]

The first major break with this traditional idea of revelation
came from the Reform Movement in Judaism. Gunther Plaut, an
influential rabbi within the movement, greatly influenced contemporary thinking. He wrote:

> God reveals Himself not only in the majesty, beauty and
> orderliness of nature, but also in the vision of moral
> striving of the human spirit. Revelation is a continuous
> process, confined to no one group and to no one age.
> Yet the people of Israel, through its prophets and sages,
> achieved unique insight in the realm of religious truth.
> The Torah both written and oral, enshrines Israel's ever-
> growing consciousness of God and of the moral law.[70]

It is quite apparent that the Reform Jewish interpretation of
revelation conflicts with the traditional position. For Reform Judaism, revelation is no longer something that flows down from God
to man. Revelation comes about through the insight and discovery
of man. Man—not God—is the author of the Bible. This idea, so
central to today's Reform Judaism, is put most succinctly by Rabbi
David Ellenson, a noted contemporary Reform scholar and former
president of the Hebrew Union College-Jewish Institute of Religion Reform seminary.

> I have great respect for the *halakhic* tradition, the tradi-
> tion of the rabbis in the first through sixth centuries, the
> medieval Jewish tradition whether it be in Byzantium or
> North Africa or Europe. But the way in which I come to
> look at it from my Reform perspective is that I see it as an
> ongoing narrative where each generation of Jews writes a
> different story in which they attempt to capture what it is
> they feel that God commands in their age.[71]

69. M. D. Tendler, in Editors of *Commentary Magazine, Condition of Jewish
Belief*, 236.

70. Plaut, *Growth of Reform Judaism*, 97.

71. Ellenson, "What Makes Me a Reform Jew?"

There is a third, unique view of revelation, that opposes both the traditional and the Reform views. The major spokesperson for this position was the great scholar Martin Buber, whose works are important in their own right. Will Herberg, an influential Jewish scholar, was profoundly influenced by Buber. He presents this "third conception of revelation":

> Revelation is not the communication of infallible information, as the fundamentalists claim, nor is it the outpouring of "inspired" sages and poets, as the modernists conceive it. Revelation is the self-disclosure of God in his dealings with the world. Scripture is thus not itself revelation but a humanly mediated record of revelation. It is a story composed of many strands and fragments, each arising in its own time, place and circumstances. Yet it is essentially one, for it is throughout the history of the encounter of God and man in the history of Israel. Scripture as revelation is not a compendium of recondite information or metaphysical propositions; it is quite literally *Heilegeschichte*, redemptive history.[72]

Buber presents his position on revelation in this famous passage: "My own belief in revelation . . . does not mean that I believe that finished statements about God were handed down from heaven to earth. Rather it means that the human substance is melted by the spiritual fire which visits it, and there now breaks forth from it a word, a statement, which is human in its meaning and form, human conception and human speech, and yet witnesses to Him who stimulated it and to His will."[73]

In his classic work on Buber's thought, Maurice Friedman offers great insight into Buber's understanding of revelation. "Revelation is thus man's encounter with God's presence rather than information about His essence. Buber rejects the either-or of revelation as objective or subjective in favor of the understanding of revelation as dialogical. To be revelation and not just literature it

72. Herberg, *Judaism and Modern Man*, 246.
73. Buber, *Eclipse of God*, 135.

must come from outside man, but that does not mean that man has no part in the form which it takes."[74]

Heschel, however, differs from these three views of revelation, even though there is a great deal of similarity among his, Buber's, and the traditional view. Still, he differs substantially. Heschel's thought contrasts most radically with the Reform notion that man discovers the truths of God. In a famous statement that reminds one of the Swiss theologian Karl Barth, Heschel exclaims: "The Bible is primarily not man's vision of God but God's vision of man. The Bible is not man's theology but God's anthropology. . . . He is not the object of a discovery but the subject of revelation."[75]

Heschel emphasizes this idea throughout his works. In *God in Search of Man*, he writes: "God's search of man, not man's quest for God was conceived to have been the main event in Israel's history. . . . Israel's religion originated in the initiative of God rather than in the efforts of man . . . . Man would not have known Him if He had not approached man. God's relation to man precedes man's relation to Him."[76] Rabbi Allan Lazaroff drew my attention to this, pointing out that "classical Judaism is both God-man and man-God. Abraham was described in the Midrash as searching for God and so became the paradigm for medieval philosophers."[77]

In many ways, Judah Halevi was a forerunner of Heschel in this formulation. In the Midrash, there are numerous accounts of Abraham's discovering God through reason without the aid of revelation. One account asks how old Abraham was when he recognized his creator. R. Hanina and R. Johanan agreed, saying that when he was forty-eight, Abraham recognized God.[78] For Louis Ginzberg, the great midrashic scholar, "It is noteworthy that in all the sources stress is laid upon the fact that Abraham came to know God through his own reasoning about the universe and its

---

74. Friedman, *Martin Buber*, 246.

75. Heschel, *MNA*, 129.

76. Heschel, *GSM*, 198

77. This was a comment made on my PhD thesis.

78. Freedman and Simon, *Midrash Rabbah*, 9:251

ruler who must necessarily exist."[79] Medieval Jewish philosophers admired Abraham not only as a prophet, but also as a philosopher who discovered God through "speculation and reasoning." Moses Maimonides states that Abraham claimed "that speculation and reasoning had come to him indicating to him that the world as a whole was a deity."[80]

With regard to the idea that reason alone was sufficient to reach God, Maimonides was preceded by Saadia (882–942), who is considered the father of medieval Jewish philosophy of religion. The scholar Julius Guttman writes: "According to him, Saadia, the Jewish religion, revealed by God, is radically different from all other religions, which are merely the work of men and thus falsely claim divine origin. However, the content of this truly divine revelation is identical in Saadia's eyes with the content of reason . . . reason is capable of reaching through its own powers the content of the divine truth."[81]

There is not uniformity among the medieval scholars, but Heschel's statement that "Israel's religion originated in the initiative of God rather than in the efforts of man" is fully in accordance with the arguments of Judah Halevi. Halevi, opposing Saadia's view, claims: "The approach to God is only possible through the medium of God's command, and there is no road to the knowledge of the commands of God except by way of prophecy, but not by means of speculation and reasoning."[82] According to Guttman, "Halevi's final and decisive objection is based on the nature of the religious relationship itself. Philosophy claims that human reason is capable, by its own powers, of finding the way toward communion with God. This contradicts the nature of the religious relationship, which is initiated by God alone; only God can show the path whereby man achieves communion with him."[83]

79. Ginzberg, *Legends of the Jews*, 217.
80. Maimonides, *Guide of the Perplexed*, bk. 1, ch. 63, p. 153.
81. Guttman, *Philosophies of Judaism*, 71.
82. Halevi, *Book of Kuzari*, 162.
83. Halevi, *Book of Kuzari*, 140.

Heschel was also influenced by the thinking of Don Isaac Abravanel (1437–1508) and Judah Lowe of Prague (1512–1609), both of whom support Halevi's position. Abravanel writes: "The Law of Moses does not include philosophical theories or logical investigations, or proofs involving high inquiries. For man's success is above Reason, and outside the sphere of Nature . . . therefore the poet said, 'I selected the way of Faith,' and 'I hated theorizing.'"[84]

Regarding Judah Lowe of Prague's position on reason and revelation, this statement by Ben Zion Bokser captures his thinking:

> Reason will guide a man in the affairs of this world but that is its limit. It does not shed enough light to illumine our faith toward God. The most important knowledge a man needs is how to live, and that cannot be attained by purely rational aids alone. "There isn't the power in the light which is reason to illumine the faith on which one must walk toward his Creator. . . This matter is above the competence of reason." We are saved from total ignorance on these matters through the fact that the "Lord revealed his ways to Moses and then to the prophets and our wise men have received the tradition from them and conveyed it to us."[85]

The Gaon has been especially influential through the ages. The scholar Louis Jacobs points out that "every Jew in the post-emancipation era, insofar as he strove to remain Jewishly committed, was a disciple of the Gaon Elijah of Vilna or the Ba'al Shem, or Mendelssohn."[86] It should be noted that, among these three, only Mendelssohn believed that man could attain eternal truths by human reason.

There is an affinity between Heschel's and Buber's approach to revelation. Both agree that revelation must be viewed as a dialogue between the prophet and God. Both also believe that the prophet is "not a passive recipient."[87] But Heschel has a problem

84. Quoted by Netanyahu, *Don Isaac Abravanel*, 292.

85. Bokser, *From the World of the Cabbalah*, 106–7.

86. Jacobs, *Encyclopedia Judaica*, 10:394.

87. Jacobs, *Encyclopedia Judaica*, 10:259.

with Buber's contention that "the laws of the Bible are only the human response to revelation and, therefore, are not binding on future generations." For Buber: "The core of revelation is not the communication of content but the event of God's presence."[88]

Heschel's view of revelation as both an event and binding content on all future generations brings him much closer to traditional Judaism than either the Reform or Buberian viewpoints. Yet, Heschel's view of revelation is not acceptable to Modern Orthodox Judaism. That's because they reject his idea that the Bible contains within itself not only the divine but, additionally, a human element.

These thoughts are extremely important in explaining Heschel's philosophy here.

> The prophet is not a passive recipient, a recording instrument, affected from without, without participation of heart and will, nor is he a person who acquires his vision by his own strength and labor. The prophet's personality is rather a unity of inspiration and experience, invasion and response . . . .
>
> Even in the moment of the event he is, we are told, an active partner in the event. His response to what is disclosed to him turns revelation into a dialogue. In a sense, prophecy consists of a revelation of God and a co-revelation of man . . . . Thus the Bible is more than the word of God: it is the word of God and man; a record of both revelation and response.[89]

Heschel's thinking contrasts radically with the traditional view, especially regarding the Five Books of Moses that comprise the Hebrew Bible, which are believed to have been dictated by God to Moses. For those modern Jews who are aware of the critical theories of the biblical scholars and cannot dismiss them as irrelevant, Heschel's view of revelation is far more satisfying.

But Heschel does not present his view because it is more in accord with modern thought. He believes it is a correct view held

88. Fackenheim, "Martin Buber's Concept of Revelation," 290.
89. Heschel, *GSM*, 269–70.

by some of the Talmudic rabbis. His two-volume Hebrew work *Theology of Ancient Judaism* challenges the idea that rabbinic Judaism is monolithic, that there is one essential stream in rabbinic thought. For Heschel, there were two major trends running through the Rabbinic tradition, the rationalistic trend, represented in the school of Rabbi Ishmael, and the mystical trend, represented in the school of Rabbi Akiva.

One issue over which these two scholars argued was the meaning of revelation. Heschel points out where the two schools stand regarding this essential concept. "In the school of Rabbi Akiva it was held that everything is in the hands of God. The Torah in all its details is given from above, and the prophet is only a vessel who receives the inspiration. In opposition to this view the school of Rabbi Ishmael taught that there were things that Moses said on his own; the prophet is a partner in prophecy not just a vessel."[90]

Heschel feels that the rationalistic school of ancient Judaism did not accept the conclusion of Rabbi Akiva with regard to revelation. The role of Rabbi Akiva is key here, having overtaken Rabbi Ishmael's thinking through the ages. Heschel insists that "Rabbi Akiba's view is known to all of us; Rabbi Ishmael's view is forgotten."[91] This statement may also be applied regarding the prophets' role in revelation. Heschel underscores a crucial idea regarding Rabbi Akiva. He feels that the Jewish tradition has forgotten Akiva's insistence that not only does God need man, but that he suffers along with the suffering of man, that God is a God of pathos.

Reviewing Heschel's book *The Prophets*, Maurice Friedman considers Heschel's "theology of pathos . . . . One of the most significant original contributions to biblical thought in our times."[92] This is an argument with which I greatly concur.

The Prophets may be divided into two major parts corresponding to the objective aspect of the prophetic consciousness of God and to the subjective aspect. Heschel summarizes what this

90. Heschel, *Theology of Ancient Judaism*, 1:iv–v.

91. Heschel, "Idols in the Temples," in *IF*, 54.

92. Friedman, "Review of *The Prophets*," 117.

implies, providing essential ideas to consider. "The objective aspect may be properly designated as the theme of prophetic theology; the subjective aspect may be designated as the theme of prophetic religion. The fundamental feature of divine reality, present in the prophets' consciousness, we have described as pathos. Their attitude or response to that reality we have found to be sympathy."[93]

Divine pathos and prophetic sympathy are not separable. The knowledge of the pathos of God by the prophets evokes the prophets' sympathy. "Any kind of sympathy with God presupposes some sort of Knowledge of the nature or of the pathos of God."[94] Heschel's idea of prophecy can be summarized this way: God calls on a prophet because of *his* pathos, and the prophet realizes the pathos of God *after* he is called and responds with sympathy.

Religion of sympathy is the awareness by the prophet of God's pathos. "There is in this relationship a direct correspondence between the divine pathos and the human sympathy, the character of the latter depending upon the character of the former. The prophet remains conscious of the fact that his feeling is a fellow feeling with God."[95]

This concept does not imply non-dualism or pantheism. It is not the *tat tvam asi* of the Upanishads, where there is an identification of the self with the Brahman. Nor is it like the *fana* of Sufism, which implies merging with God. "There is no fusion of being, *unio mystica*, but an intimate harmony in will and feeling, a state that may be called *unio sympathetica*."[96]

Let's probe more deeply into Heschel's central idea here in *The Prophets*—into "the God of pathos." "Man is not only an image of God; he is a perpetual concern of God . . . . Whatever man does affects not only his own life, but also the life of God insofar as it is directed to man."[97] Heschel finds this relation between God and man a paradox, but a paradox found in the Bible itself. "The

93. Heschel, *P*, 307.
94. Heschel, *P*, 311.
95. Heschel, *P*, 314.
96. Heschel, *P*, 319.
97. Heschel, *P*, 319.

Biblical writers were aware of the paradox involved in God's relation to man. 'Behold, to the Lord your God belong the heavens and the heaven of heavens, the earth with all that is in it; yet the Lord set his heart in love upon your fathers and chose their descendants after them, you above all peoples, as at this day.' (Deuteronomy 10:14–15)."[98]

Heschel believes that "all prophecy is one great exclamation; God is not indifferent to evil! He is always concerned; He is personally affected by what man does to man. He is a God of pathos."[99]

Modern Orthodox Jewish thinkers, following in the footsteps of the religious rationalism of Maimonides, have attacked Heschel's idea that God needs man and is affected by human actions. One example is provided by the philosopher Leon Roth, who was profoundly influenced by Maimonides, employing his *Guide for the Perplexed* as his own guide. He is severely critical of Heschel's contention that God needs man, although he does not mention Heschel by name. Roth writes:

> This doctrine, however much it can be propped up by references in the classical literature, may fairly be called a revolt. It runs counter to the basic assumption of Judaism as represented by the more obvious statements of the Hebrew Bible, the Talmudic Rabbis, the systematic account of Judaism given by the philosophers and the plain teaching of the traditional prayer book. The Pentateuch says: "Be ye holy for I the Lord your God am holy": and the old Rabbinic commentary states squarely: "If you make yourselves holy, I consider it as if you made me holy. Yet do not understand from this that IF you hallow me, I am hallowed, but if you do NOT hallow me, I am not hallowed. 'I am holy,' whether you hallow me or whether you do not."[100]

Leon Roth's position must be considered seriously, since he is a profound student of Jewish philosophy. Even Fritz A. Rothschild,

98. Heschel, *P*, 319.

99. Heschel, *P*, 284.

100. Roth, *Judaism*, 149.

the major Jewish defender of Heschel's thought, tells us that "the notion of a God of pathos whose chief characteristic is concern for and participation in the lives of his creatures is diametrically opposed to the mainstream[s] of Jewish, Moslem and Christian metaphysical theology throughout the last two millennia."[101]

Therefore, it doesn't surprise Rothschild that there is much opposition to Heschel's concept of the God of pathos. He notes: "Surely a thinker who has thrown down the gauntlet to the whole venerable tradition of Jewish and Christian metaphysical theology which includes Philo, Saadia Gaon and Maimonides . . . must expect brickbats from many directions. To replace Aristotle's Unmoved Mover with the Bible's Most Moved Mover and to argue for an anthropopathic God against the Rambam's austerely demythologized Deity is no minor matter."[102]

However, Roth's position—viewing Judaism from the perspective of Maimonides—while still very influential today, does not do justice to the true nature of Judaism. While looking at the Bible from the viewpoint of Maimonides, it dismisses as unauthentic the reading of the Bible from Rabbi Akiva's or Nachmanides's point of view as well as the Zohar and other major Jewish sources. Nachmanides, for examples, writes: "For in the plain sense of things it would appear that the dwelling of the Divine Glory in Israel was to fulfill a want below, but it is not so. It fulfilled a want above, being rather similar in thought to that which the Scripture states, 'Israel, in whom I will be glorified.'"[103]

Neither J. Abelson nor Gershom Scholem, the two great students of Jewish mysticism, bear out Roth's contention. In his introduction to the Zohar, Abelson writes: "The Moreh-Nebuchim of Maimonides was the great Jewish philosophical exposition in the Middle Ages of the 'supremacy of reason' in Judaism. But the Jew in the mass knew it not. It was never a people's book. But the Zohar was a people's book."[104]

101. Rothschild, *Between God and Man*, 26.

102. Rothschild, "Religious Thought of Abraham Heschel," 19–20.

103. Nachmanides, *Commentary on the Torah: Exodus*, 506.

104. Abelson, *Zohar*, 1:26.

Gershom Scholem agrees. "The mystics, for all their aristocratic tendencies, were the true representatives of the living popular religion of the masses, and that the secret of their success is to be found in this fact."[105]

While Roth's rabbinic source states that God is not affected by man's actions, Heschel brings us to a rabbinic source that claims the opposite. "'You are my witnesses says God and I am God,' says Rabbi Shimon Ben Yochai, the disciple of Rabbi Akiva: 'If you are my witnesses, I am God; if you are not my witnesses, I am not God.'"[106]

But the most sustained attack against Heschel's theology of pathos comes from Professor Eliezer Berkovits, who claims that this is a Christian idea with no basis in Jewish thought. Berkovits's major argument is that a God of pathos is not tenable unless it could be "reconciled with the idea of an infinite, perfect being."[107] Berkovits joins Maimonides in rejecting the idea that God needs man. A God who is perfect cannot need anything, but according to Heschel, the idea of God as a perfect being is a product of Greek philosophy, not prophetic religion. Heschel writes, "We have never been told, 'Hear, O Israel, God is perfect!'"[108]

Just as the biblical writers were aware of the paradox involved in God's relation to man, so does Heschel recognize this as a paradox. He writes: "This is the mysterious paradox of Biblical faith: God is pursuing man."[109] Heschel admits that a God of pathos is a paradox, but is it not also to be expected that a God who created the world would be involved in it? There is a question here that Heschel can ask Dr. Berkovits and other critics: "Is it more compatible with our conception of the grandeur of God to claim that He is emotionally blind to the misery of man rather than profoundly moved?"[110]

<hr>

105. Scholem, *Major Trends in Jewish Mysticism*, 229.

106. Heschel, "Teaching Jewish Theology," 17.

107. Berkovits, "Dr. A. J. Heschel's Theology of Pathos," 95.

108. Heschel, *P*, 274.

109. Heschel, *GSM*, 136.

110. Heschel, *P*, 257.

Berkovits does not attempt an answer, but he is aware of this paradox within Judaism. "This episode of a 'theology of pathos' in Judaism may, however, serve one useful purpose. It may point to the vital challenge that confronts contemporary Jewish theology. God is Infinite and Absolute and Perfect; yet, according to Judaism, the infinite, absolute, and perfect God is related to the world and cares for his creation. How are the two aspects of Divine Reality to be related to each other?"[111] Berkovits offers no solution here. He even admits that Herschel at least has undertaken to confront the challenge.

By returning to Dr. Berkovits's first objection, that a God of pathos has no basis in Judaism, Heschel finds evidence of God suffering multiple times in Isaiah. "In all their affliction, He was afflicted" (Isa 63:9). Also, "For a long time I have kept silent. I have kept still and restrained Myself; Now I will cry out like a woman in travail. I will grasp and pant" (Isa 42:14).

Heschel comments that "the allusion to the Lord as 'a woman in travail,' the boldest figure used by any prophet, conveys not only the sense of supreme urgency of His action, but also a sense of the deep intensity of His suffering."[112]

Heschel introduces other Jewish sources to make his point.

> When Israel performs the will of the Omnipresent, they add strength to the heavenly power; as it is said. "To God we render strength!" When, however, Israel does not perform the will of the Omnipresent, they weaken—if it is possible to say so—the great power of Him who is above; as it is written "Thou didst weaken the Rock that begot thee." (Deut. 32:18)
>
> And "The Holy One, as it were, said: When Israel is worthy below, my power prevails in the universe; but when Israel is found to be unworthy, she weakens my power above."[113]

111. Berkovits, "Dr. A. J. Heschel's Theology of Pathos," 102.

112. Heschel, *P*, 151.

113. Quoted by Abraham J. Heschel, "Mystical Element in Judaism," in Finkelstein, *Jews*, 1:604–5.

These sources, the first rabbinic and the second from the Zohar, show that man's actions do have an impact on God himself. Views of revelation and prophecy are therefore dependent on this critical problem: What is the nature of God? Whether we choose Maimonides's concept of a perfect God or Heschel's God of pathos, we still face a paradox. Heschel is aware of this. "It is true," he writes, "that His concern is, to most of us, one of the most baffling mysteries, but it is just as true that to those whose life is open to God His care and love are a constant experience."[114]

Yet even as Heschel's understanding of revelation is more authentic to Judaism that the medieval or "Hellenized" Jewish theology, there remain great limitations realized by Heschel as he indicates in this statement: "The goal of our 'examination' of the prophets was not to furnish the prophets with a letter of recommendation, but rather to point to the difficulty of an outright rejection of their claims. Proofs cannot open the gates of mystery for all men to behold. The only thing we can do is to open the gates of our own soul for God to behold us, to open the gates of our minds and to respond to the words of the prophets."[115]

The paths to God through the Bible and through the study of Torah are extremely difficult. For those who are not yet ready "to open the gates of our minds and to respond to the words of the prophets," Heschel offers a different path to the presence of God, through holy deeds.

114. Heschel, *MNA*, 144.
115. Heschel, *GSM*, 233–34.

4

The Path to God through Holy Deeds

As we have seen, Heschel believes there are several paths through which we can open ourselves to God. For Heschel, if you are open to the holy dimension, aware of the presence of the ineffable, and willing to experience revelation as a reality, you will find a Judaism of love and a religion of yoke—or obligation—that enhances our lives. "The first thing a Jew is told is: You can't let yourself go; get into harness, carry the yoke of the Kingdom of Heaven . . . . The predominant feature of Jewish teaching throughout the ages is a sense of constant obligation."[1]

We are obligated to God not only in our thinking, but in our daily lives. Heschel repeatedly emphasizes that Judaism is a way of thinking *and* living.[2] Heschel is best known for his study of the inner life of the pious person, but he is also true to the Jewish tradition in emphasizing that there is no division between one's inner spirituality and outward actions. Indeed, for Heschel, one's

1. Heschel, "Religion in a Free Society," in *IF*, 13.
2. Heschel, *GSM*, 197.

spiritual life is determined by concrete actions. He writes: "The Bible insists that God is concerned with everydayness with the trivialities of life."[3]

For Heschel, Judaism is the "theology of the common deed,"[4] a religion of concrete action. The path to God through the world and the word are not sufficient unless they lead the Jew to the sacred act. Heschel considers this "supreme question" for the Jew: "What does God demand of us?"[5]

Heschel, true to the Jewish tradition, states that "man is above all a commanded being, a being of whom demands may be made."[6] He continues:

> Religion has been defined as a feeling of absolute dependence. We come closer to an understanding of religion by defining one of its roots as a sense of personal indebtedness. God is not only a power we depend on. He is a God who demands. Religion begins with the certainty that something is asked of us, that there are ends which are in need of us . . .
>
> The soul is endowed with a sense of indebtedness, and wonder, awe, and fear unlock that sense of indebtedness. Wonder is the state of our being asked. . . . We are driven by an awareness that something is asked of us, that we are asked to wonder, to revere, to think, and *to live in a way compatible with the grandeur and mystery of living.*[7]

Heschel's explanation here allows us to perceive the interrelationship between the different aspect of his "path to God." The path begins with our response to the world with wonder and awe; this, in turn leads to action, to the performance of sacred deeds. Heschel continues: "Sacred deeds are designed to make living

3. Heschel, "White Man on Trial," in *IF*, 102.

4. Heschel, "White Man on Trial," in *IF*, 102.

5. Heschel, *GSM*, 168.

6. Heschel, *WM*, 107.

7. Heschel, *WM*, 109–10 (emphasis added).

compatible with our sense of the ineffable. The *mitzvot* are forms of expressing in deeds the appreciation of the ineffable."[8]

In his movement from the ineffable to *mitzvot*, Heschel makes what Maurice Friedman terms "the transition from his general philosophy of religion to his specific philosophy of Judaism."[9]

Heschel develops the third aspect of his path, the way to God through the sacred deed, in his book *Man's Quest for God* and in the third part of his major work, *God in Search of Man*, in the section titled "Response." This is Heschel's "philosophy of Judaism." It is in this third aspect that Heschel addresses himself specifically to the modern Jew.

How does Heschel understand "Response"? Here, he means worship of God (*avodat Ha-Bore*), encompassing all the commandments (*mitzvot*), including prayer. He believes that the modern Jew who begins to sense the ineffable both in the Bible and the world will respond with worship. Nevertheless, he is well aware of the difficulty faced by us in our world today in opening our eyes to the presence of God—in the world and in the Bible. Regarding the Bible, Heschel writes: "This generation does not know how to study nor what to study. We have lost the way that leads us to the Bible. We do not learn how to sense the presence of God in the words of the Bible."[10]

For those of us in the modern world who have come to grips with the first two paths but still cannot open our eyes, Heschel presents a very challenging and provocative claim. He contends that the *mitzvot*, the performance of the commandments, *are not merely our response to the demands of God. They may also serve as a path to God's presence.* In fact, Heschel's belief that we, in our modernity, are callous to the mystery of existence and detached from the biblical tradition is precisely what causes Heschel to insist that the way through deeds may be our last hope. The incredible significance he attaches to sacred deeds is even more apparent here: "A Jew is asked to take *a leap of action* rather than *a leap of thought.*

8. Heschel, *GSM*, 350 (emphasis added).

9. Friedman, "Liberal Judaism," 24.

10. Heschel, "Israel and Diaspora," in *IF*, 220.

He is asked to surpass his needs, to do more than he understands in order to understand more than he does. In carrying out the words of the Torah he is ushered into the presence of spiritual meaning. Through the ecstasy of deeds he learns to be certain of the hereness of God. Right living is a way to right thinking."[11]

Later in this text, Heschel explains in more depth why the Jew is asked to take a "leap of action": "[T]he *mitzvah* is a supreme course of *religious insight* and experience. The way to God is a way of God, and the *mitzvah* is a way of God, a way where the self-evidence of the Holy is disclosed . . . . *A mitzvah is where God and man meet.* . . . [T]o meet Him means to come upon an inner certainty of His realness, upon an awareness of His will. Such a meeting, such presence we experience in deeds."[12]

Heschel's contention that "the *mitzvah* is a supreme source of religious insight" helps us better understand the interrelationship between the three different aspects of his "path to God." The outline of *God in Search of Man* leads us to believe that the path moves from the ineffable to the reality of revelation, and then to worship. Here, however, the direction of the path is reversed. The *mitzvot* may lead us to sense the ineffable, then to the study of Torah.

Some contemporary Jewish thinkers, including Marvin Fox and Maurice Friedman, while receptive to Heschel's thought and even praising his work, find this "leap of action" problematic. I have already touched on the problem of polarity in Judaism, especially the tension between *halacha* and *aggadah*. To understand the criticism of Friedman more fully, we must recapitulate Heschel's understanding of this issue. Here, Heschel captures this tension in Judaism: "Judaism is faced with a dilemma, with a conflict between two requirements: the loyalty to the order and the requirement of *kavanah*."[13]

More than any other Jewish thinker in the twentieth century, Heschel devoted his energies to bringing *aggadah* back to its rightful place in Judaism by insisting that *aggadah* "stresses the

11. Heschel, *GSM*, 283 (emphasis added).

12. Heschel, *GSM*, 312 (emphasis added).

13. Heschel, *MQG*, 35.

spirit, *kavanah*, dedication, purity."[14] Heschel criticizes those who regard the law as the essence of Judaism, reminding us that "the fact remains that, central as is law, only a small part of the Bible deals with the law. The narratives of the Bible are as holy as its legal portions."[15] In fact, in a class lecture at Jewish Theological Seminary on October 14, 1971, Heschel was critical of the entire past 1,500 years of Judaism, for its stress on *halacha* at the expense of *aggadah*. He pointed out that there is no *halacha* in Psalms whatsoever.

Is it conceivable that Heschel, the man of *aggadah*, is asking us to take a "leap of action" before we attain inner devotion? Is he telling us to perform actions even when we don't feel the obligation to do so and can't perform them with *kavanah*? This is the problem that Friedman finds in Heschel's "leap of action."

Friedman argues: "But if we who are not observant Jews do not *now* feel ourselves commanded by God to perform the law, how can we perform it with integrity even on the strength of Heschel's assurance that we *shall* know this to be God's will for us through our observance?"[16]

This problem is even more intense for the modern Jew who wants to believe that there is a God in the world but isn't able—yet—to make the leap of faith. Is Heschel also speaking to that Jew when he considers a "leap of action"?

I think so. There is no doubt that Heschel was a master of the entire range of Jewish tradition. He was well aware of the view found in rabbinic and medieval sources that, without *kavanah*, the performance of the *mitzvot* are worthless. He even quotes the extreme view found in the Talmud, "the Rabbis call a person who performs a commandment without the proper intention a transgressor."[17] Heschel, in opposition to this rabbinic source, and to many other great Jewish scholars (e.g., Bahya ben Yosef ibn

14. Heschel, *GSM*, 338.

15. Heschel, *GSM*, 324.

16. Friedman, "Liberal Judaism," 24 (emphasis added).

17. Heschel, *GSM*, 408n2.

Paquda), tells us to perform the *mitzvot* even if we do not feel the intention at the time.

The modern Jew should take the "leap of action," even if they do not feel able—yet—to take a "leap of faith." Heschel understands that this position has difficulties. "There can be acts of piety without faith. Faith is vision, sensitivity and attachment to God; piety is an attempt to attain such sensitivity and attachment. The gates of faith are not ajar, but the *mitzvah* is a key. By living as Jews we may attain our faith as Jews. We do not have faith because of deeds; we may attain faith through sacred deeds."[18]

"Judaism insists upon the deed and hopes for the intention . . . . While constantly keeping the goal in mind, we are taught that one must continue to observe the law even when one is not ready to fulfill it 'for the sake of God.' For the good, even if it is not done for its own sake, will teach us eventually how to act for the sake of God."[19]

Heschel would agree with Friedman that the Jew who does not feel commanded by God to perform the *mitzvot* does not perform them with integrity. Yet despite the lack of integrity, Heschel insists upon the "leap of action." An examination of his important article, "Confusion of Good and Evil," focuses clearly on this problem, addressing the question of integrity itself in a new way. Profoundly influenced by kabbalistic and Hasidic thought, Heschel argues that even the saint cannot perform the commandments with complete integrity. To support his contention, he cites the Jewish mystical view "that in this world neither good nor evil exists in purity, and that there is no good without the admixture of evil nor evil without the admixture of good."[20]

This view of the nature of man was appropriated by the Hasidic movement, as exemplified in the Baal Shem Tov's interpretation, commenting on a verse of the Bible. "'For there is not a righteous man upon the earth, that does good and sins not' (Ecclesiastes 7:20). The commentators take this verse to mean that even a

18. Heschel, *GSM*, 282.

19. Heschel, *GSM*, 403–4; and "Confusion of Good and Evil," in *IF*, 140–41.

20. Heschel, "Confusion of Good and Evil," in *IF*, 134.

righteous man sins on occasion, suggesting that his life is a mosaic of perfect deeds with a few sins strewn about. The Baal Shem, however, reads the verse: *'For there is not a righteous man upon earth that does good and there is no sin in the good.'"*[21]

Heschel examines this issue from the point of view of self-interest. He asks: "If an act of good must be done exclusively for the sake of God, are we ever able to do the good?"[22] His answer is that although our deeds may never become perfect, never entirely free of self-interest, there is still great value in their performance and in our struggle to attain greater integrity. This explains Heschel's position clearly: "This, then, seems to be the attitude of Judaism. Though deeply aware of how impure and imperfect all our deeds are, the fact of our doing is cherished as the highest privilege, as a source of joy, as that which endows life with ultimate preciousness. . . . [T]he validity of the good remains regardless of all impurity."[23]

I think that Heschel's claim is somewhat of an exaggeration. As shown earlier, a similar view was not acceptable to rabbinic and medieval Judaism. But Heschel's views do have traditional supporters among some Hasidic masters, who have profoundly influenced Heschel's thought. Aaron of Starosselje, the disciple of Schneur Zalman of Liadi, who founded Chabad Hasidism, claimed that this was precisely the view of his master:

"My teacher, his soul is in Eden, further expounded the verse: 'My dove, my undefiled' (Cant. 6:9). He interpreted the word *yonah* (dove), as if it were an expression denoting 'fraud' (*'ona'ah*). No one, said he, need be apprehensive that his worship is fraudulent, containing an admixture of good and evil, for even if it is fraudulent it is still undefiled."[24]

The Hasidic masters were addressing themselves to Jews who had difficult in attaining the proper intention, even though they felt themselves commanded by God. This view does not answer the entire question of the integrity of human actions considered

21. Heschel, "Confusion of Good and Evil," in *IF*, 139 (emphasis added).
22. Heschel, "Confusion of Good and Evil," in *IF*, 140.
23. Heschel, "Confusion of Good and Evil," in *IF*, 142.
24. Quoted by Jacobs, *Seeker of Unity*, 117.

by Dr. Friedman. His concern is with the Jews who do not feel commanded by God and therefore cannot even begin to perform the commandments with integrity. In spite of this difference, Heschel, extremely critical of what he terms "religious behaviorism," attacks the "theology of respect for tradition." Yet, he insists that the contemporary Jew take this "leap of action."

Heschel has a reason for this position. He is aware of the fact that a majority of Jews today live in a Christian world and that the stress of Christianity is on love rather than on yoke, on faith rather than action. He writes: "Paul waged a passionate battle against the power of law and proclaimed instead the religion of grace. Law, he claimed, cannot conquer sin, nor can righteousness be attained through works of law. A man is justified 'by faith without the deeds of law.'"[25]

Heschel criticizes the doctrine of salvation by faith alone in an article "Protestant Renewal: A Jewish View," specifically written for *The Christian Century*. He admonishes: "Do not sell salvation too cheaply."[26] Heschel is bold enough to be critical of Christianity because he believes that the doctrine of salvation by faith conflicts with the Hebrew Bible, which is a treasure to Christianity as well as to Judaism. Therefore, he writes: "The first word in God's approach to man is: 'The Lord God commanded the man . . . . ' (Genesis 2:16). It is the commandment we must first listen to."[27]

Heschel continues to stress his opposition to Paul's doctrine. He knows that Jews today are susceptive to a tendency to elevate the spiritual at the expense of practical actions. Finally, though, Heschel realizes that the danger to contemporary Judaism today is not the performing of *mitzvot* without proper intention, but rather the complete neglect of the *mitzvot*. Therefore, he places his greatest emphasis on the performance of the deed, regardless of the intention.[28] In this, he can find agreement from the Lubavitcher Hasidim. People in New York City and elsewhere are doubtless

25. Heschel, *GSM*, 293.

26. Heschel, "Protestant Renewal: Jewish View," in *IF*, 175.

27. Heschel, "Protestant Renewal: Jewish View," in *IF*, 174–75.

28. Heschel, *GSM*, 293.

familiar with the solicitations that Lubavitchers do on street corners, asking people if they are Jewish and offering to pray with them. The leaders of this movement are certainly aware that the Jews who are picked up on the streets and encouraged to put on a pair of *tefillin* to pray or to take a set of Shabbat candles to light at home will not do so with *kavanah*. Apparently, they believe, along with Heschel, that the repeated performance of this action may eventually lead to true intention.

Others also have critical reactions to Heschel's ideas on the third way to God. Marvin Fox writes: "This, too, is a road which can lead to religious conviction only if it presupposes some measure of such conviction. If a man performs deeds without any sense of their spiritual significance whatsoever how can they be effective in leading him to God? . . . Without the commitment of faith a man is most unlikely to undertake performance of 'sacred deeds,' and if he should they will be mere posturing without any spiritual effect."[29]

Rabbi Dudley Weinberg holds a similar position, when he considers the phenomenon of prayer: "How utterly appropriate is the inscription so frequently inscribed over the ark in our synagogues: *Da lifne mee atta homed*—'Know before Whom you stand.' Without this recognition prayer can never occur. Introspection may occur; we may engage in psychological self-examination; we may study liturgical texts and even find them interesting as sources of stimulating ideas; but prayer cannot occur."[30]

Heschel appears never to have responded directly to the serious challenges posed by Fox and Weinberg. However, indirectly, he responds in statements throughout his works. Heschel's contention is that the *mitzvah* is itself a key to faith, while Fox and Weinberg present an either/or position. You either "know before whom you stand" or you do not. Yet, they seem to ignore those Jews, especially here in America, who are still searching, American Jews who are struggling to attain the knowledge that will lead them to belief.

29. Fox, "Heschel, Intuition, and the *Halakhah*," 9.
30. Weinberg, "Efficacy of Prayer," 124.

Heschel's position becomes much stronger when we realize that his "leap of action" may itself be the key to a knowledge of God. After all, Heschel especially held Jewish American youth in high regard and had hopes for a regeneration of Judaism through the power that comes from a "leap of action." Heschel writes: "American Jewish youth is one of the wonders of Jewish history. There is a simplicity of spirit, a readiness for reverence."[31] Although Heschel feels that most are not ready for what he calls "the supreme acquiescence," many young Jews are eager to perform *mitzvot* with commitment. This is a confirmation of his believe in a "leap of action."

It's likely that even Heschel, during his lifetime, could not have imagined the impact that the notion of "*tikkun olam*," repairing the world, would have on so many American Jews and especially younger Jews. To do good and to engage with social justice efforts in the name of Judaism is a cornerstone ideology especially among liberal American Jewry today. Whether they continue on their journey or not, they are engaging Jewishly in the world as Heschel envisioned—either as a first step or something more extensive. Heschel's influence and insistence on the "leap of action" is hugely responsible for this phenomenon in contemporary American Jewry. Indeed, the debate has shifted to precisely the point that Heschel examines. Is the call to action an end game or is it the beginning of a journey toward deeper spiritual engagement? Heschel, who placed preeminence on prayer, would not see the practice of *tikkun olam* as enough, though there is no doubt that the extraordinary emphasis on it in contemporary Jewish life is directly related to Heschel's influence. While this book deals with Heschel's theology, Heschel's lifetime of activism is well documented.[32]

Meanwhile, Dr. Fox is critical not only of Heschel's third way to God; he also finds fault with Heschel's first and second ways. "The Jew who is perplexed and searching is our special concern . . . Instead of being asked to look for evidence of God in

31. Heschel, "Israel and Diaspora," in *IF*, 219.

32. This book is devoted solely to Heschel's "life of action," his political engagement: *Abraham Joshua Heschel: A Life of Radical Amazement* by Julian Zelizer. See also Mort, "'To Conquer Callousness.'"

nature or in the Bible, he must be confronted with the greatest of all challenges—the challenge to find meaning in his own life. He must be forced to see that without God and His Torah men are reduced to being animals and automata."[33]

It is rather surprising that Dr. Fox, a scholar with a good comprehension of Heschel's writings, overlooks the fact that throughout all of Heschel's works, he is indeed concerned with precisely this question of the meaning of human life. Heschel states repeatedly that "our effort must involve a total reorientation about the nature of man and the world."[34] Heschel is especially concerned with the authentic Jewish concept of man. Heschel's most important statement about man and God in fact reveals the role of *mitzvot* in Judaism. In a lecture to Jewish educators, he stated:

> If you were to ask me as to what I should teach first to young people about Jewish theology, I would say teach the concept of man. I have often suggested that the Bible is a book about man. It is not a book about God. It depicts God's anthropology, rather than man's theology. The central issue in the Bible is man. Unless we understand the essential Biblical claims concerning man, we cannot teach Jewish theology. What is the essential claim? To put it in a very minimal form, it is the infinite importance of man; what man can do and how man shall act.[35]

Judaism believes that there is duality in the nature of man. Man is created from dust and, at the same time, he is made in the image of God. Heschel emphatically emphasizes the "evil" nature of man, but he nevertheless insists that the fundamental statement about man, according to Jewish tradition, is found in this passage from Genesis: "And God said: Let us make man in our image (*tselem*), after our likeness (*demuth*) . . . And God created man in His image, in the image of God created He him.' (Genesis 1:26ff)."[36]

33. Fox, "Heschel, Intuition, and the *Halakhah*," 10.

34. Heschel, "Religion in a Free Society," in *IF*, 20.

35. Heschel, "Teaching Jewish Theology," 8.

36. Abraham J. Heschel, "Concept of Man in Jewish Thought," in Radhakrishnan and Raju, *Concept of Man*, 126.

With this in mind, Heschel claims that we can now "understand the meaning of the astonishing commandment: 'You shall be holy, for I, the Lord your God, am holy.' (Leviticus 19:2)."[37]

This is all preliminary to Heschel's main theological contention about Judaism: "If I would have to make a statement about God, one that is fundamental in Judaism, it would be that God is in search of man .... If I were to summarize all of human history as seen in the Bible it would be a simple formula: 'God in search of man.'"[38]

Heschel believes that God is in search of man because "Man is needed, he is a need of God."[39]

While it is true that Heschel's postulation here raises many concerns for a range of Jewish thinkers, Heschel firmly believes that his ideas agree with biblical and rabbinic thought and are especially stressed by the Jewish mystics.[40] He writes: "Jewish mystics are inspired by a bold and dangerously paradoxical idea that not only is God necessary to man but that man is also necessary to God to the unfolding of His plans in this world."[41]

For Heschel, "life is a partnership of God and man." He says "this is why human life is holy. It is at this moment that we are able to comprehend fully not only why God entered into a 'marriage contract' with Israel but also the importance of *mitzvot*; the mitzvot are the way that the 'partnership', the 'marriage contract' between Israel and God are fulfilled."[42]

37. Abraham J. Heschel, "Concept of Man in Jewish Thought," in Radhakrishnan and Raju, *Concept of Man*, 132.

38. Heschel, "Teaching Jewish Theology," 10.

39. Heschel, "Sacred Image of Man," *IF*, 160.

40. I draw the reader's attention to the discussion in the previous chapter of this book, where we examined at some length the ideas of the Jewish scholars who criticize Heschel's ideas. The ideas are repeated here to show their implications for prayer.

41. Abraham J. Heschel, "Mystical Element in Judaism," in Finkelstein, *Jews*, 1:604.

42. For an excellent discussion of this "marriage contract," see Petuchowski, *Ever Since Sinai.*

In addition to the aspect of worship that involves the performance of holy deeds, the other two aspects of worship are study of Torah and prayer. Since the rabbinic tradition considers prayer a commandment, Heschel deals with prayer in the third aspect of his three-fold path.

Any study of Judaism reveals that the highest aspect of worship was assigned to the study of Torah. Here is a supporting statement from the Talmud: "Raba saw R. Hammuna prolonging his prayers. Said he, 'They forsake eternal life—study of the Torah—and occupy themselves with temporal life prayers.'"[43]

Although study takes precedence over prayer, there was a tendency by some rabbis to assign an equal, if not more important, role to prayer. Heschel stated: "The presence of God is found in many ways, but above all God is found in the words of the Bible."[44] This seems to give preeminence to the study of the Bible as the ideal way to encounter God's presence. Heschel agrees with the traditional view of Judaism, that study is more important than prayer.

Other statements by Heschel, especially "it [prayer] is the queen of all commandments,"[45] seem to indicate that he agrees with the Hasidic notion that prayer stands higher even than study of Torah. In this, the Hasidim were innovators. "The Hasidic elevation of prayer over other religious duties, even over that of study of the Torah, is not in keeping with the Jewish tradition. The Hasidim here were innovators," stressed Dr. Jacobs, and I concur.[46] There may be a conflict for Heschel because he never resolved this tension between study and prayer. More likely, though, he probably considered both of these aspects of worship as equal. As Dr. Friedman has pointed out, Heschel has a tendency "to stress now one point of view and now another."[47]

43. Shabbath 10a.

44. Heschel in conversation with Patrick Granfield; Granfield, *Theologians at Work*, 77.

45. Heschel, *MQG*, 69.

46. Jacobs, *Hasidic Prayer*, 17.

47. Friedman, "Abraham Joshua Heschel: Philosopher," 12.

If, as Heschel asserts in a much-quoted phrase, prayer is in fact the "queen of all commandments," we must comprehend its immense importance in Judaism. This leads us to question what, indeed, is the purpose of worship. This is, I believe, the most essential question in the Jewish tradition. We find this response in the Midrash: "Rab said: The precepts were given only in order that men might be refined by them. For what does the holy One, blessed be he, care whether a man kills an animal by the throat or by the nape of its neck? Hence its purpose is to refine [try] man."[48]

Louis Jacobs helps us understand what is really at stake here, the traditional Jewish position regarding "reasons for the Commandments." He writes: "The meaning of this Midrashic passage seems to be that the deed in itself can have no significance so far as God is concerned, but it is the effect of the deed on the human character that he wants. The command to slaughter animals in this way rather than that, at the neck rather than at the back of the neck, has as its aim the inculcation of kindness and compassion. By slaughtering animals in the most painless way rather than by cruel methods man's character becomes refined."[49]

According to this Midrash, then, God requires us to "do justly ... love mercy and walk humbly with our God" (Mic 6:8), and the element of divine worship enters when man fulfills these requirements. Worship is the way for man to keep his evil inclinations in check, a way which constantly reminds him that there is a God in the world.

Maimonides and Nachmanides both agree with this essential thesis, that worship is for man's sake and not for God's. Maimonides writes: "Know that all the practices of the worship, such as reading the Torah, prayer, and the performance of the other commandments, have only the end of training you to occupy yourself with His commandments ... rather than with matters pertaining to this world; you should act as if you were occupied with Him . . . . And not with that which is other than He."[50]

48. Freedman and Simon, *Midrash Rabbah*, 1:361.

49. Jacobs, *Jewish Theology*, 1183.

50. Maimonides, *Guide of the Perplexed*, bk. 3, ch. 51, p. 622.

Maimonides himself strongly opposed the idea that God needs man's worship. After all, a god who is perfect is not in need of anything. But man must worship God to overcome his strong attachment to material things. By occupying ourselves with God's commandments, we suppress our evil inclinations and live up to God's will.

Nachmanides, who believed, uniquely, that prayer is not commanded by God,[51] also stressed that prayer is for the sake of man rather than for the sake of God. He wrote: "The advantage which results from the observance of the precepts is not to God Himself, may he be exalted, but the advantage is to man himself, to keep him far from harm or from evil beliefs or from ugly character traits or to remind him of the wonders of the Creator, blessed be He, so that man might know God."[52]

The kabbalistic view of prayer may be seen in the following statement by the great Jewish mystic Isaiah Horowitz (ca. 1565–1630). He writes: "It is not enough for man to carry out the precepts and serve God in all that He has commanded with joy and good heart. In addition he should become a 'chariot' for God that from his worship the needs of the Most High should be satisfied, the Name perfected, and the King united with His Glory. This is the ultimate purpose of worship, for the needs of the Most High."[53]

This clearly claims that the ultimate aim of worship is for the sake of God, so that "the King may be united with His Glory."

The notion that God needs man's worship, that "the very harmony of the upper worlds depends on man's worship," is set forth by the Lithuanian mystic Alexander Susskind of Grodno (d. 1793), who taught that "the main intention of the Creator, blessed be He, and His main purpose in creation, is for the sake of man, *that he might by his worship give satisfaction to God,* blessed be His name. Happy is the man who fears the Lord and delights exceedingly in His commandments. Who is mighty upon earth to perfect the upper worlds by His thought and utterance all the days of his life in

51. Heschel, *MQG*, 67.

52. Quoted by Jacobs, *Jewish Theology*, 184.

53. Jacobs, *Jewish Theology*, 185.

this world. This note is sufficient for the intelligent."[54] If, by "the intelligent," Susskind means those who understand that God needs man's worship, then Heschel would perfectly fit that description.

Heschel consistently repeats the idea that God needs man. We can interpret this to mean that God needs man's worship. Heschel argues that, even in Talmudic times, the rabbis debated whether or not God needs the worship of man. One view is that man, who is "flesh and blood needs God, but God does not need the worship of flesh and blood." Another view claims that "God needs our worship; the righteous man gives strength to God."[55]

There are many statements in the Midrash that support Heschel's argument that there were rabbis in Talmudic times who emphasized God's need for human worship. Here is one example: "Why were the matriarchs barren? R. Levi said in R. Shila's name and R. Helbo in R. Johanan's name: Because the Holy One, blessed be He, yearns for their prayers and supplications."[56]

For Heschel, worship has great power precisely because it is God who needs man's prayers. He explains: "Moreover, we must not overlook one of the profound principles of Judaism. There is something which is far greater than my desire to pray, namely God's desire that I pray . . . . How insignificant is the outpouring of my soul in the midst of this great universe! Unless it is the will of God that I pray, unless God desires our prayers, how ludicrous is all my praying."[57]

Heschel revels in the power of prayer and the observance of the *mitzvot*, because this expands God's presence in the world. "Great is the power of prayer. For to worship is to expand the presence of God in the world. God is transcendent, but our worship makes Him immanent. This is implied in the idea that God is in need of man: His being immanent depends upon us."[58]

---

54. Quoted by Jacobs, *Principles of the Jewish Faith*, 156.

55. Heschel, *Theology of Ancient Judaism*, 1:76. My translation from the Hebrew original (emphasis added).

56. Freedman and Simon, *Midrash Rabbah*, 1:381.

57. Heschel, *MQG*, 58.

58. Heschel, *MQG*, 62.

5

The Religious Significance of Abraham Joshua Heschel

Heschel is established as one of the most significant religious figures of our time. His books *Man Is Not Alone* (1951) and *God in Search of Man* (1955) were incredibly influential. His entire legacy—the writing and the living—expanded his influence. As his reputation grew, some Jews began to call him the Zaddik, the saint of our generation, while some scholars diverged from this opinion—Ben-Horin, Berkovits, Arthur Cohen, to name a few, were severe critics of Heschel's thought. Even friendly critics like Maurice Friedman and Eugene Borowitz disagreed with many of Heschel's ideas at various points. But it would be difficult for anyone to deny that Heschel's thought is influential not only among Jewish scholars, but among Jewish youth. *The American Jewish Yearbook of 1968* reported that 25 percent of Jewish theological seminary students chose Heschel as the rabbi "who best reflects their own religious-philosophical-theological position." And, for rabbis and rabbinical students ordained by the Hebrew Union College Jewish Institute of Religion of the Reform Movement, the largest movement denomination of Judaism in the US, and where he once taught, he has only gained more importance through the decades.

Some Christian thinkers started to consider him the prophet of the times.[1] Reinhold Niebuhr's prediction made in 1951 came true: Heschel indeed became to many the "commanding and authoritative voice not only in the Jewish community but in the religious life of America."[2]

A not inconsequential part of Heschel's legacy is that, for the first time in American history, both Jews and Christians looked to a Jewish scholar in New York for guidance. Christians began to view Judaism with new respect. W. D. Davies, a prominent Christian scholar, writes, "I speak for Christians and other non-Jews. To encounter him [Heschel] was to 'feel' the force and spirit of Judaism, the depth and grandeur of it."[3]

A. J. Sanders gave this assessment: "I have no doubt whatever that Abraham Joshua Heschel was Jewish, Jewish to the very core of his being, a truly contemporary Hasid. But, in all his Jewishness, Heschel was a *shalia la-goyim*, an apostle to the gentiles . . . . His influence on Christianity, especially since the publication in 1951 of *The Sabbath* and *Man Is Not Alone*, has been remarkable."[4]

Even Heschel's most severe critics could not deny that he had mastered the whole of Judaism and that what he said about his own tradition held an important message for Jews and Christians, alike. Heschel's' vast knowledge enabled him to shatter a number of long-standing, false ideas held by some Jews and Christians, especially the critical one that there is no Jewish theology or that the rabbis were not concerned with theological issues. "Theology, it is claimed, is alien to Judaism; the law, 'an ox who gores a cow,' is Jewish theology, for Judaism is law and nothing else." This view, in the words of Heschel, "maintains that, according to Judaism, there

1. Victor M. Perez Valera wrote, "Heschel was a scholar, a theologian, an author; he was above all a prophet." Valera, "Religious Experience," 4.

2. Niebuhr, "Masterly Analysis of Faith."

3. Davies, "Conscience, Scholar, Witness," 214.

4. Sanders, "Apostle to the Gentiles," 61.

is only one way in which the will of God need be fulfilled, namely, outward action; that inner devotion is not indigenous to Judaism; that Judaism is concerned with deeds, not with ideas; that all it asks for is obedience to the law."[5]

Heschel's emphasis on "wonder," "awe," and "inner devotion" became the grounds by which Judaism could no longer be dismissed as primarily a dry religion of law opposed to enthusiasm and mysticism. It could no longer be easily argued that the "Jewish mind and character, in spite of its deeply religious bent, was alien to mysticism." There was of course a long Jewish mystical tradition, but most non-Jewish scholars simply failed to study the vast ethical and mystical literature of the Jews. This notion that Judaism is opposed to mysticism was not the creation of Christian scholars only, but it was advocated too by a group of Jewish writers including Graetz, Zunz, and Geiger, whose treatment of mysticism was not sympathetic in the least.[6]

Heschel's presentation of Judaism stirred the hearts and minds of both Jews and Christians because he incorporated into his own system of thought many of the insights of the Jewish mystical tradition. He seized upon an idea central to Jewish mysticism when he wrote that "Jewish mystics are inspired by a bold and dangerously paradoxical idea that not only is God necessary to man but that *man is also necessary to God*, to the unfolding of His plans in this world."[7] Heschel asks: "Who is in need of man?" He answers: "Man is needed, he is a *need of God*."[8]

Heschel believed in a God of pathos, as we have cited, and importantly, that God needs our prayers. These ideas were originally advocated by Jewish mystics like Rabbi Akiva and others,

5. Sanders, "Apostle to the Gentiles," 320. For a classical presentation of the inwardness in Judaism see the previously cited Ibn Paquda, *Duties of the Heart*; also, Luzzatto, *Mesillat Yesharim*.

6. Inge, *Christian Mysticism*, 39. Compare Graetz, *History of the Jews*, 4:625, *et passim*; Scholem, *Major Trends in Jewish Mysticism*; and Abraham J. Heschel, "Mystical Element in Judaism," in Finkelstein, *Jews*, 1:602–23.

7. Abraham J. Heschel, "Mystical Element in Judaism," in Finkelstein, *Jews*, 1:604 (emphasis added).

8. Heschel, *MNA*, 215.

though ultimately they were rejected by Jewish rationalists like Rabbi Ishmael and Maimonides. Heschel's constant insistence that reason alone is insufficient in our quest for God, his stress "that in matters that concern the totality of life, all higher attainments of our personality should be brought into play, particularly our sense of the ineffable," again points to Heschel's mystical inclination.[9] By constantly using the term "ineffable," Heschel stimulated a number of Christian and Jewish writers to point out Heschel's affinity with mysticism in general. For example, Hal Bridges writes that "the ineffable" recalls the first of William James's four marks of mystical experience, ineffability.[10]

Meanwhile, Jakob Petuchowski sees Heschel as a mystic because of his "constant harping on the 'ineffable,' his almost compulsive return to the theme of awe and wonder, his frequent disquisitions on the sublime."[11] Hasidic influence was crucial on Heschel's thinking. And it behooves us to remember that Hasidism, itself, was a revival of a Jewish mystical tradition which accepted not only the Zohar but the Lurianic Kabbalah "as a revelation of divine truth." It helps, here, to keep in mind a statement about the Hasidic masters (with which Heschel would agree): "[T]he temperament and individuality of the various Zaddikim determined the use to which the mystical literature of Israel should be placed."[12] Additionally, Heschel points out that, unlike the Baal Shem Tov, the Kotzker Rebbe "opposed the study of Kabbalah: since he felt that one should first struggle with the 'confusion in his own soul' before devoting time to a study of the 'mysteries of the world on high.'"[13]

But Heschel's interest in the mystical element of Judaism dates back even further than Hasidism. He cites the Hebrew Bible as a source of early Jewish longing for immediate contact with the divine. "Not all of the people of the Bible are satisfied with awareness of God's power and presence. There are those 'that seek Him, that

9. Heschel, *MNA*, 56.

10. Bridges, *American Mysticism*, 62.

11. Petuchowski, "Faith as the Leap of Action," 391.

12. Newman, *Hasidic Anthology*, xviii.

13. Heschel, *PT*, 79.

seek Thy face O God of Jacob' (Psalms 24:6) . . . At Sinai, according to legend, Israel was not content to receive the divine words through an intermediary. They said to Moses, 'We want to hear the words of our King from Himself . . . We want to see our King.'"[14]

Heschel continues by quoting from Judah Halevi (b. ca. 1080), who lived before the Zohar was written. Halevi says: "To see the face of my King is my sole desire. I fear none but Him; I revere only Him. Would that I might see Him in a dream! I would continue to sleep for all eternity. Would that I might behold His face within my heart! Mine eyes would never ask to look at anything else."[15]

Most Jewish scholars from the nineteenth century through to today, either the "rational" school or the "Orthodox" tradition, have ignored the major insights of the Jewish mystical tradition. They have even viewed the Kabbalah "as essentially un-Jewish."[16] However, Heschel incorporates essential mystical material into all aspects of his path to God. He shows that God can be "as real as life" and that Jewish kabbalists "want to feel and to enjoy Him; not only to obey, but to approach Him."[17] Heschel uses mystical writings from sources as diverse as the Psalms to the Baal Shem Tov to address himself to contemporary religious questions. He is able to speak relevantly about mysticism.

Harvey Cox, the well-regarded Baptist scholar, observed that "we are so afraid of the emotional element in religion that we may have pushed people in search of the numinous to look elsewhere."[18] This, at a time, when the drug culture was prevalent, and Heschel was able to speak precisely to this by citing human needs. "I interpret the escape to drugs as coming from the need for experiencing moments of exaltation. Man is in need of relaxation,

---

14. Heschel, *GSM*, 28–29.

15. Heschel, *GSM*, 29.

16. Wijnhoven, "Gershon G. Scholem," 468.

17. Abraham J. Heschel, "Mystical Element in Judaism," in Finkelstein, *Jews*, 1:602.

18. Cox, "God and the Hippies."

but he is also in need of exaltation. He cannot live on sedatives alone. He is in vital need of stimulants."[19]

For Heschel, "the classical Jewish form of exaltation is worship. Prayer lifts a person above himself."[20] In a clear espousal of Jewish mystical views, he also stresses that "to worship God is to forget the self."[21]

However, it wouldn't be fair to label Heschel simply as a mystic. Heschel explains: "I am trying to form a synthesis between the mystical thought of Rabbi Akiva and the rationalistic thought of Rabbi Ishmael. You can't just follow Jewish mysticism or Jewish rationalism. You need a synthesis."[22] While the label "mystic" is insufficient in describing Heschel, his bringing this Jewish mystical tradition to the forefront is perhaps a central reason for the fact that the Christian world has noticed him as they have. In fact, the only other major Jewish thinker in the twentieth century to elicit such a response in the Christian world was Martin Buber. Like Heschel, he was profoundly influenced by the mystical movement of Hasidism. For Heschel and for Buber both: "The path to Jewish mysticism lies through the service of one's fellow men; it cannot be over-emphasized that to the Jew mysticism did not mean eschewing this world in the selfish concern with personal salvation."[23]

Heschel, who, during his lifetime, became as well-known for his activism as for his theology, was true to this mystical tradition of service to others when he spoke out against the "moral outrage of Vietnam." One of these times was in the US Capitol on January 31, 1967. "At this hour, Vietnam is our most urgent, our most disturbing religious problem, a challenge to the whole nation as well as a challenge to every one of us as individuals . . . Vietnam

19. Heschel, "Man's Search for Faith," 14.

20. Heschel, "Man's Search for Faith," 14.

21. Heschel, *MQG*, XIII.

22. Heschel, in a lecture to his rabbinical students at the Jewish Theological Seminary, New York, Dec. 1971.

23. Wolk, "Mysticism," 1:76.

is a personal problem. To speak about God and remain silent on Vietnam is blasphemous."[24]

It is perhaps no accident, too, that when he spoke out about Viet Nam in other instances, he did so, in a church setting, at Riverside Church. He was a founder of Clergy and Laity Concerned About Vietnam, with Rev. Daniel Berrigan, his brother Philip Berrigan, and Rev. William Sloane Coffin (whose Riverside Church was the center of anti-war activity). And he played a leading role in the Civil Rights Movement, marching along with prominent Reform and Conservative rabbis with Martin Luther King in Selma, Alabama.[25]

The impact Heschel made on Christian theologians went beyond their joint activism, without doubt. Why did a scholar and teacher, so authentically Jewish, make such an impact on the Christian world?

Key to this impact is how Heschel's "path to God" is meaningful to Christianity.

Heschel's first path, man's path to God through the world, which he develops in *Man Is Not Alone* and the first part of *God in Search of Man*, is directed as much to Christianity as to Judaism. His concern is not particular to Jewish beliefs. He wants to open our eyes to the holy dimension, the realm of the ineffable, equally meaningful to Jews and Christians. Heschel's work *Man Is Not Alone* provoked this response from John C. Bennett, the former president of Union Theological Seminary. It shows the impact that Heschel had on some of the most influential religious figures in America. Bennett was obviously struck by the mystical element in Heschel.

"In that book and in others that followed, his words had the *power to evoke experiences of wonder and awe, awareness of the transcendence of the divine and the uniqueness and depth of the human.* He was never intimidated by the prevailing secularizing of religious positions, but he announced, and he embodied, the dimensions of experience which that secularizing trend neglected. He helped

---

24. Abraham J. Heschel, "Moral Outrage of Vietnam," in Brown et al., *Vietnam Crises of Conscience*, 49.

25. Mort, "'To Conquer Callousness.'"

people to see, as he said, that 'the loss of awe is the great block to insight,' that 'a return to reverence is the first prerequisite for a revival of wisdom, for the discovery of the world as an allusion to God' that phrase, 'the world as an allusion to God,' says so much."[26]

Heschel's impact on the Christian world rests most profoundly with the second aspect of his path, the way to God through the Bible. Heschel argued that not only the Jew, but also the Christian, can encounter the presence of God through studying the Hebrew Bible. For Heschel, "An ultimate decision for Jew or Christian is whether to be involved in the Hebrew Bible or to live away from it. The future of the Western world will depend on the way in which we relate ourselves to the Hebrew Bible."[27]

Heschel's attempts to prove the reliability of the prophets and the reality of revelation, and his attempt to comprehend the prophet's experience of God as a God who is concerned with the world, a God of pathos who suffers with the world, was received enthusiastically by many important Christian thinkers. For instance, Franklin Sherman notes Heschel's great contribution to biblical thought with his "notion of divine pathos." He sees affinity between Heschel, Hartshorne, and Kierkegaard. He claims that Heschel expounded biblical materials more thoroughly than the other thinkers. Sherman also asserts that Heschel's "divine Pathos" is "more believable than is the concept of an unmoved mover or a distant cosmic principle."[28] Another scholar, Norman Gottwald, stressed that "*The Prophets* should be widely used in Bible and philosophy of religion courses. It is a volume with appetizers for the beginner and meaty rewards for the connoisseur. To read it is to experience what the author has experienced in reading prophecy—'a ceaseless shattering of indifference.'"[29]

Heschel's influence on the Christian world can best be seen in this editorial from *America*, the notable Jesuit publication.

---

26. Bennett, "Agent of God's Compassion," 205 (emphasis added).

27. Heschel, "Protestant Renewal," in *IF*, 168–70.

28. Sherman, *Promise of Heschel*, 35–36.

29. Gottwald, "Review of Heschel's *The Prophets*," 190.

There was, in one sense, nothing out of the ordinary in the remarks that Pope Paul VI addressed to a crowd gathered at the Vatican in a general audience on January 31, 1973. The Holy Father spoke eloquently and in familiar terms about the nature of man's quest for God. Toward the end of those remarks he reminded his hearers that "even before we have moved in search of God, God has come in search of us." It was not those words that caught the attention of the world press, however, but the fact that the subsequently published text of the papal talk cited the writings of Abraham Joshua Heschel as the source of that thought. This citation of the 1968 French edition of *God in Search of Man* was, in the memory of veteran observers of the Roman scene, an unprecedented public reference by a pope to a writer who was not a Christian.[30]

Heschel must have realized that his works on the Bible were having influence. During the International Theological Conference at the University of Notre Dame, Heschel commented: "[A]s a person who prays for the spiritual health and integrity of Christians, I am particularly delighted with the new emphasis upon the study of the Hebrew Bible. I think the renewal of biblical studies encouraged by the document on scripture is to me, as a Jew, of equal importance. All I would like to see is that the world should open its mind and heart to the words of the prophets and then there will be no need for documents on Jews or others."[31]

Unlike the first two aspects of Heschel's path, his third path, the way to God through the commandments, is addressed primarily to Jews. While Heschel, as a friend of the Christian world, is at times critical of Christianity, feeling that "the need within Protestantism for re-examination, revision and renewal is of extreme urgency,"[32] this should not be interpreted to mean that Heschel wants Christians to observe the Jewish commandments. This would imply that for Heschel there is only one true way to God,

30. Editorial, "Contemporary Judaism and the Christian," 202.

31. Abraham J. Heschel, in Miller, *Vatican II*, 373–74.

32. Heschel, "Protestant Renewal: Jewish View," in *IF*, 175.

which is the complete opposite of his spirit. He writes: "Is it not blasphemous to say: I alone have all the truth and the grace, and all those who differ live in darkness, and are abandoned by the grace of God?"[33]

Heschel's contribution to an understanding of the Jewish commandment to prayer was noticed by the Christian world. In reviewing Heschel's *Man's Quest for God*, a work largely devoted to prayer, a theologian known for his teachings on the importance of prayer, Charles Whiston, writes:

> This book will speak deeply to us all, Christian or Jew, concerning a much neglected area of religious life—the life of prayer. Very few books have ever been written in the field of prayer, seeing so clearly the theological dimensions and grounding of praying. . . . This book may well turn out to be the most important book dealing with the theology of praying that has been published in our time. To read it is to find one's own life deeply and piercingly judged—by God . . . it is good to sit at the feet of Dr. Heschel, truly a man of prayer.[34]

In another influential review of *Man's Quest for God*, the Catholic scholar Eldon M. Talley writes: "If it were possible to say that the wisdom which is Israel has come to its finest contemporary flowering in the works of Rabbi Heschel, at least to my mind, this collection of his studies and meditations on prayer and symbolism is the most beautiful."[35]

Any consideration of Heschel's impact on the Christian world must begin with Heschel's "depth theology." Charging that "theology has often suffered from a preoccupation with dogma, the content of believing," Heschel proposes the alternative depth theology as "the act of believing." He argues persuasively for a new theological purpose, for a theology that explores the depths of faith, "the sub-stratum out of which belief arises." For "theology is

33. Heschel, "No Religion Is an Island," 126.
34. Whiston, "Review of Heschel's *Man's Quest for God*," 315.
35. Talley, "Wisdom of Heschel," 360.

in the books; depth theology is in the hearts. . . . Theologies divide us; depth theology unites us."[36]

The implication of this is obvious. Heschel's motive is quite clear, to begin a dialogue between Judaism and other religions, at the source where discussion is possible. While most Jewish theologians begin with theology and end with theology, Heschel begins with "depth theology."

This is the essential distinction between Heschel and other Jewish theologians writing as his contemporaries. Many great Christian theologians like Paul Tillich, Reinhold Niebuhr, and even Pope John XXIII, who no longer insisted on trying to convert the Jews to Christianity, would, I believe, have agreed with Heschel's statement: "The most fruitful level for interreligious discussion is not that of dogmatic theology but that of depth theology."[37]

Heschel's' preoccupation with depth theology did not deter him from his concern with the content of belief with Judaism. There can be no doubt that as far as any particular religion is concerned, Heschel's major preoccupation is with Judaism. But Heschel realized that the fate of Judaism in the US is bound up with the fate of Christianity. "The Jewish diaspora today, almost completely to be found in the Western World, is certainly not immune to the spiritual climate and the state of religious faith in the general society."[38]

Heschel tasked himself, therefore, with transforming the hearts and minds not only of Jews but also of Christians and of everyone. This inevitably makes him a major religious figure for Jews, of course, but also for the entire religious world.

There is another reason for Heschel's significant impact on the Christian world. We live in an ecumenical age. Interreligious relationships are vital and serious. Just as Jewish today are concerned with what the Christian world has to say about Judaism, Christians are concerned with Jewish attitudes toward their religion. Heschel has a unique and radical posture toward Christianity. He reported: "Yes, I witnessed a miracle: there came Pope

36. Heschel, "Depth Theology," in *IF*, 119.

37. Heschel, "What We Might Do Together," 138.

38. Heschel, "No Religion Is an Island," 119.

John." To my knowledge, words like this about a pope were never before uttered by a Jew.

These comments by Heschel for sure were controversial. Trude Weiss-Rosmarin, the Jewish feminist editor, took strong exception here: "I know that Rabbi Heschel is given to ecstatic language. But even when one makes allowances for this inclination, I think it is going a bit too far—considering the facts—to say, as he did; 'Yes, I witnessed a miracle: there came Pope John.'" For Weiss-Rosmarin, "the facts" seem to be that "it is inevitable that if Jewish-Christian encounters are honest and frank, hurt and insult will ensue. Theologically—and Jewish-Christian dialogues are theological dialogues—Judaism is the negation of Christianity and Christianity is the negation of Judaism. There is no bridge and no compromise between Jewish and Christian beliefs. These beliefs and affirmations are mutually exclusive—and this applies also to the God concept."[39]

Regarding this view, Eliezer Berkovits writes: "As to a dialogue in the purely theological sense, nothing could be less fruitful and more pointless. . . . Whatever is not Jewish in Christianity is not acceptable to the Jew." Berkovits offers a further reason why Jewish-Christian dialogue is impossible: at the time when he was writing, the memory of the Holocaust was still fresh. "We feel that, emotionally, we are not as yet ready to enter into a fraternal dialogue with a church, a religion, that has been responsible for fathers and mothers, brothers and sisters, in the present generation."[40]

Heschel responds to his critics with this story: The first peasant says: "You don't love me." The second peasant responds: "How do you know I don't love?" Answers the first peasant: "If you love me, you would know what ails me." The second peasant tells him: "But you never tell me what ails you. Is this not a sign that you don't love me?"

Historically, Jewish sages did not generally grant validity to other religious traditions. This, even though Judaism has expressed the belief that all men could attain salvation by following the Noachic

39. Weiss-Rosmarin, "Who's Afraid of Dialogue," 25.

40. Berkovits, *Faith after the Holocaust*, 44–45.

laws. There are some exceptions. The Yemenite Jewish scholar Nathanel ben Fayyumi granted validity to other religious traditions. The well-known Jewish Islamic scholar S. D. Goitein writes:

> In a book written in the early 1160's, Nathanel ben Fayyumi, then leader of the Jews of inland Yemen, explains that Mohammed was a true prophet and the Koran a book revealed by God, for there was constant emanation from the world of holiness to the world of matter in order to save it from Hell. Religion was like a medicine adapted by God to each nation according to its state and needs; naturally Islam was not destined for the Jews, who had been chosen by God for his special message.[41]

This does not mean that the Judaic tradition views all other religions as absolutely false. It does distinguish between its "daughter religions," Christianity and Islam, and those not connected with it in any specific way.

Louis Jacobs has captured the traditional Jewish attitude toward unrelated religions in this statement.

> The Far Eastern religions with all the profundity of thought in some of their teachings, cannot seriously be considered as rivals of Judaism. In their cruder forms they are idolatrous, in their higher forms atheistic; quite apart from their failure to eradicate cruel and immoral practices. The attitude of Judaism to its "daughter religions" is more complicated. Many Jewish authorities hold that these faiths are not idolatry so far as non-Jews are concerned—that is to say the good Christian or the good Muslim is a "saint of the nations of the world." For the Jew, however, Christianity, certainly, and Islam, possibly, are to be considered idolatrous and history informs us how many Jews gave their lives rather than embrace these faiths. Judaism rejects the claims made for both Jesus and Mohammed. It teaches that the central dogma of Christianity strikes at the roots of pure monotheism and

41. Goitein, *From the Land of Sheba*, 15. See also *Encyclopedia Judaica*, 12:971.

that Islam is both too fatalistic and has too low an ethical standard as compared with Judaism.

But this, of course is not to deny that Judaism considers that there is much of value in her daughter religions.[42]

Throughout the ages, Judaism paid little attention to the Asian religious traditions. It may have been out of ignorance, as this passage shows. In one of Judaism's most treasured books, the *Kuzari*, written by the greatest poet of medieval Judaism, Judah Halevi, there is a most interesting passage relating to Indian religion. Al Kuzari asks: "Does it not weaken thy belief if thou art told that the Indians have antiquities and buildings which they consider to be millions of years old?" The Rabbi answers: "It would, indeed, weaken my belief had they a fixed form of religion, or a book concerning which a multitude of people held the same opinion, and in which no historical discrepancy could be found. Such a book, however, does not exist. Apart from this, they are a dissolute, unreliable people, and arouse the indignation of the followers of religions through their talk, whilst they anger them with their idols, talismans, and witchcraft. To such things they pin their faith and deride those who boast of the possession of a divine book. Yet they only possess a few books, and these were written to mislead the weak-minded."[43]

The Judaic tradition does see "value in her daughter religions," but this value lies in the religious ideas these traditions share with Judaism. Though Judaism saw value in church and mosque, it nevertheless considered these religions ultimately false from God's point of view. In his Code of Jewish Law, Moses Maimonides points out another reason why Christianity and Islam are valuable. "All these events relating to Jesus and even those relating to him who succeeded the one referred to Mohammed, were nothing else than a means for preparing the way for the King Messiah."[44]

An exception to this thinking was the great Jewish scholar Franz Rosenzweig (1886–1929). Seymour Siegel, commenting on

42. Jacobs, *We Have Reason to Believe*, 133–34.

43. Halevi, *Book of Kuzari*, 46.

44. Quoted by Jacobs, *We Have Reason to Believe*, 134. See also Goldstein, *Jesus in the Jewish Tradition*, 190.

Rosenzweig's position of granting validity to Christianity, says: "Rosenzweig asserts the Christian claim that no one comes to the Father except through Jesus. He stresses that no one comes to the Father. This refers to the non-Jews who are still on the way; for Jews, who are already with the Father through the Jewish covenant, it is not necessary to come to the Father. Thus, Christianity is the Judaism of the gentiles, through which the gentiles come to know and be with the God of Israel."[45]

Rosenzweig's thoughts influenced A. Roy Eckardt, the Methodist minister who was also a pioneer in Jewish-Christian relations. Eckardt writes:

> A Christian theology of the Jewish-Christian relationship is called to proclaim from the Christian side what Franz Rosenzweig has expressed from the Jewish side: Judaism is the 'star of redemption,' Christianity the rays of that star. The church is 'successor' of Israel in only one respect and no other: by virtue of the Christian gospel, the dividing wall between Jew and Gentile is destroyed once and for all. The abiding covenant with Israel is decisively and definitely opened to the world in a way that Jewish faith does not provide.
>
> All Jews will not by any stretch of imagination ever assent to Rosenzweig's affirmation that the Gentile world is able to come to God only through Jesus Christ. But the Christian church may testify that Rosenzweig is right, although of course it will do this only from the standpoint of its own Christological persuasion.[46]

It is vital to note that Heschel's position goes beyond Rosenzweig and grants validity not only to Christianity but to all the world religions. He says specifically, "Perhaps it is the will of God that in this aeon there should be diversity in our forms of devotion and commitment to Him. In this aeon diversity of religions is the will of God."[47]

45. Seymour Siegel, in his introduction to Thomas Walker's *Jewish Views of Jesus*. See also Glatzer, *Franz Rosenzweig*, 341–42.

46. Eckardt, *Elder and Younger Brothers*, 160.

47. Heschel, "No Religion Is an Island," 126.

Heschel seems to leave little doubt that Jews, Christians, and Muslims, in their various ways, are truly worshiping God. But does this statement also apply to other world religions whose concept of God is totally different from that of the Jewish tradition? In this passage, where Heschel quotes the prophet Malachi and expands on the quote with an interpretation, he indicates that, indeed, Asian traditions are also valid to him.

> "For from the rising of the sun to its setting; My name is great among the nations, and in every place incense is offered to My name, and a pure offering; for My name is great among the nations," says the Lord of Hosts (Mal. 1:11).
>
> This statement refers undoubtedly to the contemporaries of the prophet. But who were these worshipers of One God? At the time of Malachi there was hardly a large number of proselytes. Yet the statement declares: All those who worship their gods do not know it, but they are really worshipping Me.
>
> It seems that the prophet proclaims that men all over the world, though they confess different conceptions of God, are really worshipping One God, the Father of all men, though they may not be aware of it.[48]

Indeed, Jewish scholarship in defense of Asian traditions was rare. The only one I could find was written in 1280 in Baghdad by Saʿd Ibn Mansur Ibn Kammuna. The author of this fascinating study on comparative religion writes:

> The worship of idols is in existence to this day among the Chinese, Turks, Indians, and others. True, it ceased among the Arabs with the coming of Muhammad. It has been said, however, that the Black Stone was one of the idols that was in the Ka'ba, but that, unlike the other idols, it was not removed. Muslims to this day seek closeness to God through kissing and touching the Black Stone, which is a kind of worship. The idolators do not believe idols create heaven and earth; no sensible person does. But they do feel that idol worship brings one closer

48. Heschel, "No Religion Is an Island," 127.

to God. We are informed by the Koran that they said: this is our way to bring us near to God in intimacy."[49]

This Jewish writer, who apparently is writing for Muslim intellectuals, suggests that, in spite of the obvious iconolatry of the Black Stone, Muslims are truly worshiping God; and this is also true of the Chinese, the Hindus, and others. Heschel renews this rare spirit of tolerance toward Asian religious traditions.

Heschel's interpretation of Malachi comes very close to the spirit of Hinduism exemplified in this statement by Sri Ramakrishna: "Supposing it is a mistake to worship God in the image, doesn't he know he alone is being worshipped? He will certainly be pleased by that worship."[50] It is no surprise, then, that the Center for Integrative Education, whose "main areas of interest have been the mediation of Eastern and Western thought," realized that there is some affinity between Heschel and Asian though. They asked him, in fact, to become a member of their Board of Governors.[51]

Heschel opened the door for a Jewish encounter with Asian traditions, while he also created a rich atmosphere for Jewish-Christian dialogue. His statements that "in this aeon diversity of religions is the will of God" and "men all over the world . . . are really worshipping One God"[52] were an inviting entry point to a dialogue that transformed the atmosphere among Jews and other religions.

Paul Tillich, the great Christian theologian, claimed: "A dialogue between representatives of different religions has several presuppositions. It first presupposes that both acknowledge the value of the other's religious conviction (as based ultimately on a revelatory experience) so that they consider the dialogue worthwhile."[53]

---

49. Ibn Kammuna, *Examination of the Three Faiths*, 147–48.

50. Quoted by Isherwood, *Ramakrishna and His Disciples*, 264.

51. I was given a copy of the invitation letter by Dr. Heschel. It was dated June 9, 1972.

52. Heschel, "No Religion Is an Island," 127.

53. Tillich, *World Religions*, 62.

Heschel's thinking corresponds well to this essential presupposition of Tillich. Heschel believed that it was "vitally important . . . for Judaism to reach out into non-Jewish culture in order to absorb elements which it may use for the enrichment of its life and thought."[54] While there are profound differences between Heschel's "path to God" and some of the most basic assumptions of Asian thought, Heschel's thought emphasizes his belief that Judaism could be enriched with dialogue "between the river Jordan and the river Ganges."[55]

Heschel's willingness was amazing indeed—to encounter and to be enriched by Asian thought, especially when we realize the radical distinction between Heschel's "path to God" and the ultimate goal of Asian thought. We can consider this difference looking both at Hinduism and Buddhism.

Hinduism has consistently stressed a goal of salvation, described by Professor D. S. Sarma this way:

> The Hindu Scriptures . . . teach that the ultimate end of human life is liberation (moksha) from that finite human consciousness of ours which makes us see all things as separate from one another and not as part of a whole. When a higher consciousness dawns upon us, we see the individual parts of the universe as deriving their true significance from the central unity of spirit. . . . When this goal is reached, man is lifted above his mortal plane and becomes one with that ocean of pure being, consciousness, and bliss, called Brahman in Hindu scriptures.[56]

Buddhists have repeatedly stressed that without nirvana, or enlightenment, without liberation or salvation, there is no Buddhism. Isshu Miura, the Japanese Zen master, begins his book on Zen with the statement: "The living heart of all Buddhism is enlightenment or satori."[57] With respect to enlightenment, Buddhism did not break away from Hinduism.

54. Heschel, *GSM*, 15.

55. Heschel, *GSM*, 15.

56. Sarma, "Nature and History of Hinduism," 4.

57. Miura and Sasuki, *Zen Koan*, 3.

Heschel stresses a similar form of salvation in Judaism. He insists that the central aim of the pious Jew is to encounter God, so that he realizes that he is known by God. Salvation is never for oneself; it is rather for the entire world. "Indeed, even the most personal concern, the search for meaning," Heschel tells us, "is utterly meaningless as a pursuit of personal salvation."[58]

In fact, Heschel speaks harshly about those who seek personal salvation. "Self-fulfillment is a myth which a noble mind must find degrading. All that is creative in man stems from a seed of endless discontent."[59]

There is a contrast between how the pious Jew experiences the path to God and that of the Buddhist. Heschel believes that the pious Jew is in a state of endless tension. He offers no final union of bliss for solving all of life's problems. There is, instead, a constant wrestling for "flashes of insight that 'come and go, penetrate and retreat, come forth and withdraw.'"[60]

The path to God, for Heschel, "is a continuous wrestling, a continuous being on the way to the reality and the presence of God."[61] Judaism, Heschel tells us, teaches each person "to be content with what he has, but never with what he is."[62] Heschel believes that the pious Jew can never fully and permanently attain to a static stage of what the Buddhists call nirvana, because the Jew can never fully penetrate the secret of life. We can never attain ultimate truth.

The Ceylonese Buddhist monk Walpola Rahua, meanwhile, tells us that "he who has realized the Truth, Nirvana, is the happiest being in the world. He is joyful, exultant, enjoying the pure life, his faculties pleased, free from anxiety, serene and peaceful."[63]

Heschel uniquely engaged with interfaith dialogue as a leading Jewish scholar. And, while there are other Jewish scholars who

58. Heschel, *WM*, 45.

59. Heschel, *WM*, 86.

60. Heschel, *GSM*, 132.

61. Heschel, "God of Judaism and the Christian Renewal," n. p.

62. Heschel, *MNA*, 257.

63. Rahua, *What the Buddha Taught*, 43.

encourage a Jewish-Christian dialogue, Heschel was an early and leading voice for dialogue between Jewish scholars and those who practice the Asian religions.[64]

As we consider Heschel's unique attitude toward other religions, it's important to consider two interrelated questions. The first is of great importance. Is Heschel's position in agreement with the classical sources of Judaism? The second question is critical to understanding Heschel. Is his position consistent within his own theological structure?

A central attempt that Heschel makes to use classical Jewish sources as a basis for his radical position to grant validity to all world religions is his interpretation of the passage from Malachi.[65] Heschel's view comes into direct conflict with classical sources of Judaism. It would be difficult, for example, to argue with Guttman's position that "biblical monotheism, denying the very existence of all the gods of polytheism, claimed for itself final and exclusive religious truth as given in the divine revelation."[66]

Indeed, the biblical position toward other religions is supported by rabbinic Judaism. Here, Louis Jacobs describes it:

> The Rabbis continued unabated the struggle against pagan idolatry—avodah zarah ... "strange worship," as they called it. A whole tractate of the Talmud, bearing this name, is devoted to the laws concerning total rejection of anything which smacks of idolatrous worship. The Rabbis had in mind here chiefly the Greek and Roman pantheon, but there are to be found frequent polemics, too, against Zoroastrianism, Christianity and Gnostic dualism, all of which are generally lumped together as the heresy of affirming "two powers," i.e., that there is more than one God.[67]

---

64. Another American Jewish thinker who pioneered this dialogue is Maurice Friedman. In his very moving work *Touchstones of Reality* he describes how he was enriched by his encounter with Asian thought. See *Touchstones of Reality*, especially ch. 6, pp. 85–126.

65. Malachi 1:11.

66. Guttman, *Philosophies of Judaism*, 14.

67. Jacobs, *Jewish Theology*, 285.

Jacobs goes on to explain that while Jews attacked the doctrine of the Trinity during the Middle Ages, during the rabbinic period, they attacked Christianity for its "dualism, i.e., for its doctrine of the Incarnation which Jews saw as dualistic in content, a belief in god the Father and Jesus the Son as 'two powers.'"[68]

In fact, during the Middle Ages, biblical and rabbinic Judaism advocated that Judaism was the only true religion. "There is no doubt . . . that all the medieval Jewish thinkers considered both Islam and Christianity to be false and Judaism alone the true religion."[69] Jacobs was clearly referring to major Jewish thinkers of the time. However, Jacobs was clearly not aware of the positions of Nathanel ben Fayyumi and Sa'd Ibn Mansur Ibn Kammuna, whose views would contradict Jacobs's claims.

Saadia, considered the "father of medieval Jewish philosophy of religion" and "the greatest of the Geonim," set the tone for the entire medieval period. Guttman, a major authority on this period, writes, "According to him, Saadia, the Jewish religion, revealed by God, is radically different from all other religions which are merely the work of men and thus falsely claim divine origin."[70]

S. D. Goitein clarifies Moses Maimonides's position. It's similar to Saadia's. Goitein explains: "Maimonides . . . was an uncompromisingly orthodox Jew who regarded Judaism alone as a real religion. . . . To him, Israel's religion was to be compared to a human being; all other religions are only images of a human being, beautiful images perhaps, but imitations, nevertheless. Maimonides' attitude, which was shared by most of the other Jewish thinkers who wrote in Arabic, certainly was in conformity with the Bible."[71]

Another example of this line of thinking is from the fifteenth century Jewish philosopher Abraham Bibego: "In response to the challenges of Christianity and philosophy, Bibego argued that

68. Jacobs, *Jewish Theology*, 25.

69. Jacobs, *Jewish Theology*, 286.

70. Guttman, *Philosophies of Judaism*, 71.

71. Goitein, *Jews and Arabs*, 145.

Judaism was the one, true and rational faith which brought salvation to the believers among the Jewish people."[72]

Immanuel Jakobovits, chief rabbi of Great Britain from 1967 to 1991, states the Orthodox position this way:

> As a professing Jew, I obviously consider Judaism the only true religion, just as I would expect the adherents of any other faith to defend a similar claim for their religion . . . the recognition of other faiths as "equally true" is branded an apostasy in Jewish law (Sanhedrin 63a, based on Ex. 22:19). Judaism, to be true to itself, is bound to reject, for instance, the divinity of Jesus or the prophecy of Mohammed as false claims; otherwise its own claims, such as the supremacy of Moses' prophecy and the finality of the Mosaic law . . . could not be true . . . Two mutually exclusive and conflicting statements of fact can never both be true.[73]

So it does appear that Heschel's attitude toward other religious traditions was in conflict with the position of classical Judaism. But is Heschel's attitude here consistent with his own theological structure? First, before answering, let's examine some of Heschel's most fundamental presuppositions.

Heschel's most important premise is that contemporary man lives in agony,[74] and that the "humanity of man is longer self-evident."[75] He writes: "The overriding issue of this hour in the world and Western civilization is the humanity of man. Man is losing his true image and shaping his life in the image of anti-man."[76] Supporting his point, Heschel quotes Robert Fitch's devastating description of modern man: "Man is a beast. The only difference between man and the other beasts is that man is a beast that knows he will die . . . The one irreducible value is life, which you must

72. Lazaroff, "Theology of Abraham Bibego," 3.

73. Immanuel Jakobovits, in Editors of *Commentary Magazine, Condition of Jewish Belief*, 112–13.

74. Heschel, *WM*, 27.

75. Heschel, *WM*, 25.

76. Abraham J. Heschel, "Jewish Notion of God," in Shook, *Renewal of Christian Thought*, 114.

cling to as you can and use for the pursuit of pleasure and of power. The specific ends of life are sex and money. The great passions are lust and rapacity."[77] Heschel also warns us that we should never "take lightly man's pronouncements about himself."[78]

Heschel's pessimistic view of man is echoed by Maurice Friedman, who says that "we cannot deny . . . that no matter how monstrous, misshapen, irrational, and distorted the images of man presented to us by contemporary literature and art may be, they do mirror 'significant aspects of the human condition in our time.'"[79] Will Herberg echoes this writing that man is "lost indeed, desolate and forlorn in a hostile universe."[80]

Heschel's solution to the predicament of modern man is one of his most essential presuppositions. He repeats throughout his work that paradoxical though it is, nevertheless, it is true that man is not alone—that God is concerned about man and in search of him. This is the essence, the most fundamental idea of biblical thought for Heschel, the idea that he believes has been stressed through Jewish tradition. He writes, "Paradoxical as the Bible is, we must accept its essential premise: that God is concerned about man and in search of him."[81] Therefore, for Heschel, "the renewal of man" can occur only if we come to grips with the biblical view of the world and accept its essential paradoxical premise: "that God is concerned about man."[82] Heschel pleads for us to acknowledge his argument. "All I would like to see is that the world should open its mind and hear to the words of the prophets."[83]

Will Herberg essentially agrees with Heschel on this. He believes that we would be moved out of our present day agony

---

77. Heschel, *WM*, 26–27.

78. Heschel, *WM*, 24.

79. Friedman, *To Deny Our Nothingness*, 21.

80. Herberg, *Judaism and Modern Man*, 74.

81. Abraham J. Heschel, "Jewish Notion of God," in Shook, *Renewal of Christian Thought*, 115–16.

82. Abraham J. Heschel, "Jewish Notion of God," in Shook, *Renewal of Christian Thought*, 115–16.

83. Abraham J. Heschel, in Miller, *Vatican II*, 374.

to "significant being" by accepting the biblical view of the world. Herberg writes: "Only from what is beyond life, only from the transcendent source of life, can come the power to deliver us from our desperate plight. In more traditional language, only the God whom we know to be the Creator of heaven and earth, the Lord of life and history, can help us."[84]

Herberg acknowledged along with Heschel that the world-view of Asian thought differs profoundly from the "Hebraic world-outlook," but he is consistent in his position. He levels a strong attack, therefore, on the "Greco-Oriental" religious position. For instance, in his final analysis of Buddhism, Herberg tries to show that the Buddha's preaching is a "repudiation of Buddhism." Herberg argues: "After explaining that, in the Greco-Oriental view, 'salvation is an achievement of the individual for himself and by himself,' Moore adds, 'Buddha discovered the way and taught it to men.' But why? Why, having discovered it, did he teach it to others? This question would seem to constitute an insurmountable stumbling block to Buddhism and to lead it to what in effect is a repudiation of itself."[85]

But Heschel's position is far more problematic. His essential premise is that biblical religion is the answer for the world, but he asserts, too, the validity of Asian religions by using a biblical passage from Malachi. There appears to be an inner contradiction here.

Marvin Fox writes: "Judaism is not possible without belief in the existence of God, in His absolute unity, in His revelation . . . These I hold to be true beliefs, even though not demonstrable. Any beliefs contradictory of these or of other fundamentals of Jewish faith I must, therefore, hold to be false. Simple logic forces me to this conclusion."[86]

Fox holds this view that there can't be an allowing for views other than Judaism if indeed one believes that the biblical world-view is a solution to the human problem. This appears to pinpoint

84. Herberg, *Judaism and Modern Man*, 34.

85. Herberg, *Judaism and Modern Man*, 47–57 and 79–80.

86. Marvin Fox, in Editors of *Commentary Magazine, Condition of Jewish Belief*, 65.

a logical inconsistency in Heschel. Yet, Heschel appears to have a similar position. He persistently argues that in spiritual life we must simply admit that paradox exists. We have already shown that Heschel considers his "essential premise: that God is concerned about man" to be *paradoxical.* In *The Prophets,* Heschel writes that "it is a paradox beyond compare that the eternal God is concerned with what is happening in time."[87] In another work, *Who Is Man?,* Heschel calls God's concern for man the "great puzzle."[88] Heschel does not attempt to assemble this puzzle. That's because just as his essential biblical premise is for him a "paradox beyond compare," so also is the idea that all religions are valid as paradox beyond the logic of man.

Heschel's acceptance of paradox is altogether antithetical to the mainstream of Jewish tradition, which, on the whole, maintains that religious ruth is in harmony with reason. Jewish thinkers centered their attack on the concept of the Trinity precisely because they believed that it conflicted with reason. For instance, this statement by Joseph Albo (1380–1444), the author of the popular *Sefer ha-Ikkarim,* is typical: "The law of Moses says nothing about trinity because it is not true from the point of reason."[89]

Louis Jacobs, in a discussion of paradox in the Jewish tradition, argues that although in the main, Judaism has opposed paradox, exceptions have occurred among the Jewish mystics and especially among the Hasidic masters. He shows that both Schneur Zalman of Liadi, the founder of Chabad Hasidism, and his most important disciple, Rabbi Aaron B. Moses of Starosselje, embraced paradox in religious life.[90]

Jacobs cites another concrete example:

> Another Hasidic thinker who embraces paradox as essential to faith is Rabbi Nahman of Bratzlav (1772–1811). In Rabbi Nahman's dialectic of faith doubts and difficulties are essential ingredients in the life of faith because

87. Heschel, *P,* 259.

88. Heschel, *WM,* 74.

89. Albo, *Sefer ha-Ikkarim,* 3:224.

90. Jacobs, *Faith,* 204–7.

> the finite human reason is found to come into conflict
> with the Infinite. This is endemic to man's condition as a
> finite creature. . . A god who raises no problems for hu-
> man thought would not be God for the very reason that
> the Infinite is bound to offend the finite mind.[91]

The Kotzker Rebbe (whose influence on Heschel was profound) seems to agree with the Bratzlaver. Heschel (in what must
be a free translation) quotes the Kotzker: "A God whom any Tom,
Dick, and Harry could comprehend, I would not believe in."[92]

Heschel explains: "This conception does not exclude any understanding by man of God's ways. It merely states that while some
of those ways seem absurd from man's perspective, they are none-
theless meaningful in the eyes of God. In other words, the ultimate
meaning of God's ways is not invalidated because of man's incapac-
ity to comprehend it; nor is our anguish silenced because of the
certainty that somewhere in the recesses of God an answer abides."[93]

However, his emphasis on paradox may serve as a clue to understanding why he made no serious attempt to support his position on world religions. It could also be the reasons why he made
no attempt to reconcile the apparent inner contradiction in his
own thought. Nevertheless, his position is problematic for thinkers who follow the rationalistic Jewish tradition. This is especially
true for certain very influential thinkers like Berkovits, Marvin
Fox, and Jacob Petuchowski.

Yet, Heschel's position made him an extraordinarily important figure in inter-faith dialogue. A thorough analysis of the Jewish attitude to the other religions from biblical times to the present
reveals that Heschel's position, paradoxical though it is, turns out
to be the most meaningful position of dialogue between Judaism
and other religions in our time.

Before Heschel, theological dialogue was not significant precisely because the participants did not grant validity to each other's
religions. Heschel changed all that. By accepting the validity of

91. Jacobs, *Faith*, 207.
92. Heschel, *PT*, 293.
93. Heschel, *PT*, 293.

other religious traditions, Heschel was able to find a divine element in these traditions. Heschel cites a Talmudic source that clearly supports this interpretation. "It is a well-established tradition in Jewish literature that the Lord sent prophets to the nations, and even addressed Himself directly to them."[94] According to Heschel, "The Jews do not maintain that the way of the Torah is the only way of serving God."[95]

As a passionately committed Jew, he was also revered by many Christians. The Catholic theologian John Merkle said it best: "In his own life and works, Abraham Joshua Heschel revealed the supreme importance of God as well as what it is like to live with faith in God."[96] He also played a major role in shaping the church's view of Judaism. He was the most important voice during the meeting of the Second Vatican Council (1962–65). His engagement led to historic changes in the relationship between the Catholic Church and Judaism, where the church—under Pope Paul VI—changed. This included the Church denouncing anti-Semitism and omitting any reference to conversion of the Jews.[97]

As I have shown, for Heschel, "religion is a means, not an end."[98] Heschel's "path to God," which incorporates both Jewish mysticism and rationalism, his "ecumenical spirit," his special concern for the Christian world, and his emphasis on depth theology, all contributed to his position as a major force in religious thought in America.

Heschel was one of the outstanding theologians of the twentieth century. He demonstrated that the Jew can "experience the momentous realness of God," by presenting a dimension of Judaism that challenges us in our contemporary setting to respond. As a great theologian who yearned for the transcendent, he was

94. Heschel, *P*, 226.

95. Heschel, "No Religion Is an Island," 9.

96. Kasimow, "Heschel's View of Religious Diversity," 19–25.

97. Kasimow, "Heschel's View of Religious Diversity"; and "Session VIII: Discussion," in Miller, *Vatican II*, 373.

98. Heschel in conversation with Patrick Granfield; Granfield, *Theologians at Work*, 79.

a scholar who carefully examined the riches of Judaism and made significant contributions to learning. His example is one that can guide us through the complexities of our contemporary world by offering a rich, multi-layered path to experience our Judaism and the world around us.

Bibliography

Abelson, Joshua. *The Immanence of God in Rabbinical Literature*. New York: Hermon, 1969.

———. *The Zohar*. New York and London: Soncino, 1933.

Agus, Jacob. *The Evolution of Jewish Thought: From Biblical Times to the Opening of the Modern Era*. London: Abelard-Schuman, 1959.

———. *The Vision and the Way: An Interpretation of Jewish Ethics*. New York: Frederick Ungar, 1969.

Albo, Joseph. *Sefer ha-Ikkarim*. Edited and translated by Isaac Husick. Philadelphia: JPS, 1946.

Beck, Lewis W., ed. *Eighteenth Century Philosophy*. New York: Free Press, 1966.

Bennett, John C. "Agent of God's Compassion." *America* 128:9 (Mar 10, 1973) 205–6.

Berger, Peter L. *A Rumor of Angels*. New York: Anchor, 1970.

Berkovits, Eliezer. "Dr. A. J. Heschel's Theology of Pathos." *Tradition* 6:2 (Spring 1964) 67–104.

———. *Faith after the Holocaust*. New York: Ktav, 1973.

Bokser, Ben Zion. *From the World of the Cabbalah: The Philosophy of Rabbi Judah Lowe of Prague*. New York: Philosophical Library, 1954.

Borowitz, Eugene B. "Abraham Joshua Heschel and Joseph Baer Soloveitchik: The New Orthodoxy." In *A New Jewish Theology in the Making*, 1515. Philadelphia: Westminster, 1968.

Bridges, Hal. *American Mysticism: From William James to Zen*. New York: Harper and Row, 1970.

Brown, Robert McAfee, et al. *Vietnam Crises of Conscience*. New York: Associated Press, Herder and Herder, and Behrman House, 1967.

Buber, Martin. *Eclipse of God: Studies in the Relation between Religion and Philosophy*. New York: Harper Torchbooks, 1957.

———. *Tales of the Hasidism: The Later Masters*. New York: Schocken, 1969.

Cox, Harvey. "God and the Hippies." *Playboy Magazine*, Jan 1968.

Daiches, David. "The Influence of the Bible on English Literature." In *The Jews, Their History, Culture and Religion*, edited by Louis Finkelstein, 1114. Philadelphia: JPS, 1949.

Davies, W. D. "Conscience, Scholar, Witness." *America* 128:9 (Mar 10, 1973) 213–15.

Diamond, Malcolm L. *Martin Buber: Jewish Existentialist*. New York: Harper Torchbooks, 1968.

Dubnow, S. M. *History of the Jews in Russia and Poland: From the Earliest Times until the Present Day*. 3 vols. Philadelphia: JPS, 1916.

Eckardt, A. Roy. *Elder and Younger Brothers: The Encounter of Jews and Christians*. New York: Charles Scribner's Sons, 1967.

Editorial. "Contemporary Judaism and the Christian." *America* 128:9 (Mar 1973) 202.

Editors of *Commentary Magazine*. *The Condition of Jewish Belief: A Symposium Compiled by the Editors of* Commentary Magazine. New York: Macmillan, 1966.

Efros, Israel I. *Ancient Jewish Philosophy: A Study in Metaphysics and Ethics*. Detroit: Wayne State University Press, 1964.

Ellenson, David. "What Makes Me a Reform Jew?" *College Commons Bully Pulpit* podcast (transcript), Feb 15, 2018.

Fackenheim, Emil L. "Martin Buber's Concept of Revelation." In *The Philosophy of Martin Buber*, edited by Paul Arthur Schilpp and Maurice Friedman, 273–96. La Salle, IL: Open Court, 1967.

Finkelstein, Louis, ed. *The Jews: Their History, Culture and Religion*. 2 vols. Philadelphia: JPS, 1949.

Fox, Marvin. "Heschel, Intuition, and the *Halakhah*." *Tradition* 3:1 (Fall 1960) 5–15.

Freedman, Harry, and Maurice Simon, eds. *Midrash Rabbah*. Vol. 3, *Exodus*. London: Soncino, 1961.

———. *Midrash Rabbah*. Vol. 1, *Genesis*. London: Soncino, 1961.

———. *Midrash Rabbah*. Vol. 9, *Song of Songs*. London: Soncino, 1961.

Friedman, Maurice S. "Abraham Joshua Heschel: The Philosopher of Wonder." *Congress Bi-Weekly* (Dec 18, 1967) 12–14.

———. "Abraham Joshua Heschel: Toward a Philosophy of Judaism." *Conservative Judaism* 10:2 (Winter 1956) 2.

———. "Liberal Judaism and Contemporary Jewish Thought." *Midstream* (Autumn 1959) 24.

———. *Martin Buber: The Life of Dialogue*. New York: Harper Torchbooks, 1960.

———. "Review of *The Prophets* by Heschel." *Judaism* 13:1 (1964) 117.

———. "The Thought of Abraham Heschel." *Congress Weekly* (Nov 14, 1955).

———. *To Deny Our Nothingness: Contemporary Images of Man*. New York: Delta Books, 1968.

———. *Touchstone of Reality: Existential Trust and the Community of Peace*. New York: E. P. Dutton, 1972.

Ginzberg, Louis. *The Legends of the Jews*. Philadelphia: JPS, 1947.

Glatzer, Nahum N. *Franz Rosenzweig: His Life and Thought*. New York: Schocken, 1961.

Goitein, S. D. *From the Land of Sheba: Tales of the Jews of Yemen*. New York: Schocken, 1973.

———. *Jews and Arabs: Their Contacts through the Ages*. New York: Schocken, 1967.

Goldstein, Morris. *Jesus in the Jewish Tradition*. New York: Macmillan, 1950.

Golomb, Elhanan H. *Judah Ben Solomon Campanton and His Arba'ah Kinyanim*. Philadelphia: Dropsie College for Hebrew and Cognate Learning, 1930.

Gottwald, Norman K. "Review of Heschel's *The Prophets*." *Religious Education* (Mar–Apr 1964) 190.

Graetz, Heinrich. *History of the Jews*. 6 vols. Philadelphia: JPS, 1894–1916.

Granfield, Patrick. *Theologians at Work*. New York: Macmillan, 1967.

Greeley, Andrew M. *Unsecular Man: The Persistence of Religion*. New York: Dell, 1974.

Guttman, Julius. *Philosophies of Judaism: The History of Jewish Philosophy from Biblical Times to Franz Rosenzweig*. Translated by D. W. Silverman. New York: Doubleday, 1966.

Halevi, Judah. *Book of Kuzari*. New York: Pardes, 1946.

Herberg, Will. *Judaism and Modern Man: An Interpretation of Jewish Religion*. New York: Harper Torchbooks, 1965.

Hertz, Joseph H. *The Authorized Daily Prayer Book*. New York: Block Publishing, 1961.

Heschel, Abraham J. *The Earth Is the Lord's and the Sabbath*. New York: Harper & Row, 1966.

———. *Encyclopedia Judaica*. Jerusalem: Keter 1971.

———. *God in Search of Man: A Philosophy of Judaism*. New York: Farrar, Straus & Giroux, 1955.

———. "The God of Judaism and the Christian Renewal." *The Catholic Hour*, Jan 21, 1968. N. p.

———. "Heschel's Last Words." *Jerusalem Post Magazine*, Dec 29, 1972, 13.

———. *The Insecurity of Freedom: Essays on Human Existence*. New York: Farrar, Straus and Giroux, 1966.

———. *Kotzk: The Struggle for Integrity*. Yiddish. 2 vols. Tel-Aviv: Hamenora, 1973.

———. *Man Is Not Alone: A Philosophy of Religion*. New York: Farrar, Straus, and Young, 1951.

———. *Man's Quest for God: Studies in Prayer and Symbolism*. New York: Macmillan, 1983.

———. "Man's Search for Faith." *United Synagogue Review* (Spring 1971) 14.

———. "No Religion Is an Island." *Union Seminary Quarterly* 21.2 (Jan 1966) 117–34.

———. *A Passion for Truth*. New York: Farrar, Straus & Giroux, 1973.

———. *The Prophets*. New York: Burning Bush, 1962.

———. "Reason and Revelation in Saadia's Philosophy." *The Jewish Quarterly Review* 34:4 (1944) 391–408.

———. "Teaching Jewish Theology in the Solomon Schechter Day School." *The Synagogue School* (Fall 1969) 8–17.

———. *Theology of Ancient Judaism.* Hebrew. 2 vols. London: Soncino, 1962.

———. "What We Might Do Together." *Religious Education* (Mar–Apr 1967) 135–38.

———. *Who Is Man?* Stanford, CA: Stanford University Press, 1968.

Heschel, Susannah, ed. *Moral Grandeur and Spiritual Audacity: Essays, Abraham Joshua Heschel.* New York: Farrar, Straus, and Giroux, 1996.

Holtz, Abraham. "Religion and the Arts in the Theology of Abraham Joshua Heschel." *Conservative Judaism* (Fall 1973) 27–39.

Husik, Isaac. *A History of Mediaeval Jewish Philosophy.* New York: Meridian Books, 1958.

Ibn Kammuna, Sa'd Ibn Mansur. *Ibn Kammuna's Examination of the Three Faiths.* Translated by Moshe Perlmann. Berkeley: University of California Press, 1971.

Ibn Paquda, Bahya Ben Joseph. *Duties of the Heart.* Translated by Moses Hyamson. 2 vols. Jerusalem: Boys Town Jerusalem, 1965.

Inge, William Ralph. *Christian Mysticism.* New York: Meridian, 1956.

Isherwood, Christopher. *Ramakrishna and His Disciples.* New York: Simon and Schuster, 1965.

Jacobs, Louis. *Faith.* New York: Basic Books, 1969.

———. *Hasidic Prayer.* New York: Schocken, 1973.

———. *A Jewish Theology.* New York: Behrman House, 1973.

———. "Liberal Supernaturalism." In *Varieties of Jewish Belief,* edited by Ira Eisenstein, 111–22. New York: Reconstructionist Press, 1966.

———. *Principles of the Jewish Faith: An Analytical Study.* New York: Basic Books, 1964.

———. *Seeker of Unity: The Life and Works of Aaron of Starosselje.* New York: Basic Books, 1966.

———. *We Have Reason to Believe: Some Aspects of Jewish Theology Examined in the Light of Modern Thought.* London: Vallentine, Mitchell, 1962.

Kaplan, Edward K. "Form and Content in Abraham J. Heschel's Poetic Style." *Central Conference of American Rabbis* 18 (Apr 1971) 28–39.

———. "Language and Reality in Abraham J. Heschel's Philosophy of Religion." *Journal of the American Academy of Religion* (Mar 1973) 94–111.

Kasimow, Harold. "Heschel's View of Religious Diversity." *Studies in Christian-Jewish Relations* 2:2 (2007) 19–25.

Lazaroff, Allan. "The Theology of Abraham Bibego: A Defense of the Divine Will, Knowledge and Providence in Fifteenth Century Spanish Jewish Philosophy." PhD thesis, Brandeis University, 1973.

Long, Edward LeRoy, Jr., and Robert T. Handy, eds. *Theology and Church in Times of Change.* Philadelphia: Westminster, 1970.

Luzzatto, Moses Hayyim. *Mesillat Yesharim: The Path of the Upright.* Translated by Mordecai Kaplan. Philadelphia: JPS, 1966.

Maimonides, Moses. *The Guide of the Perplexed.* Translated by Shlomo Pines. Chicago: University of Chicago Press, 1963.

McClelland, David C. *The Roots of Consciousness.* Princeton, NJ: D. Van Nostrand, 1964.

Merkle, John C. *The Genesis of Faith: The Depth Theology of Abraham Joshua Heschel.* New York: Macmillan, 1985.

Miller, John H., ed. *Vatican II: An Interfaith Appraisal.* South Bend, IN: University of Notre Dame Press, 1960.

Miura, Isshu, and Ruth Fuller Sasuki. *The Zen Koan: Its History and Use in Rinzai Zen.* New York: Harcourt, Brace & World, 1965.

Moore, George Foot. "Christian Writers on Judaism." *Harvard Theological Review* 14.3 (Jul 1921) 197–254.

———. *Judaism in the First Centuries of the Christian Era.* Cambridge: Harvard University Press, 1966.

Mort, Jo-Ann. "'To Conquer Callousness.'" *Democracy Journal* 65 (Summer 2021). https://democracyjournal.org/magazine/65/to-conquer-callousness/.

Nachmanides, Moses. *Commentary on the Torah: Exodus.* Translated by Charles B. Chavel. New York: Shilo Publishing House, 1973.

———. *Commentary on the Torah: Genesis.* Translated by Charles B. Chavel. New York: Shilo Publishing House, 1971.

Netanyahu, B. *Don Isaac Abravanel: Statesman and Philosopher.* Philadelphia: JPS, 1968.

Newman, Louis I. *The Hasidic Anthology: Tales and Teachings of the Hasidim.* New York: Schocken, 1968.

Niebuhr, Reinhold. "Masterly Analysis of Faith." *New York Herald Tribune Book Review,* Apr 1, 1951.

Petuchowski, Jakob J. *Ever Since Sinai: A Modern View of Torah.* New York: Scribe, 1968.

———. "Faith as the Leap of Action: The Theology of Abraham Joshua Heschel." *Commentary* (May 1958) 390–97.

Plaut, W. Gunther. *The Growth of Reform Judaism.* New York: World Union for Progressive Judaism, 1965.

Quebedeux, Richard. *The Young Evangelicals.* New York: Harper and Row, 1974.

Rabinowicz, Harry M. *The World of Hasidism.* Hartford: Hartmore, 1970.

Rabinowitsch, Wolf Zeev. *Lithuanian Hasidism.* New York: Schocken, 1971.

Radhakrishnan, S., and P. T. Raju, eds. *The Concept of Man: A Study in Comparative Philosophy.* Lincoln, NE: Johnson, 1960.

Rahua, Walpola. *What the Buddha Taught.* New York: Grove, 1962.

Randall, John Hermann, Jr. *The Making of the Modern Mind: A Survey of the Intellectual Background of the Present Age.* Cambridge: Riverside, 1926.

Roth, Leon. *Judaism: A Portrait.* New York: Schocken, 1972.

Rothschild, Fritz A. *Between God and Man: An Interpretation of Judaism.* New York: Free Press, 1959.

———. "The Religious Thought of Abraham Heschel." *Conservative Judaism* (Fall 1968) 19–20.

Sanders, J. A. "An Apostle to the Gentiles: A Conversation with Rabbi Abraham J. Heschel." *Conservative Judaism* (Fall 1973).

Sarachek, Joseph. *Faith and Reason: The Conflict over the Rationalism of Maimonides.* New York: Hermon, 1970.

Sarma, D. S. "The Nature and History of Hinduism." In *The Religion of the Hindus*, edited by Kenneth W. Morgan, 4. New York: Ronald Press, 1953.

Scholem, Gershom G. *Major Trends in Jewish Mysticism.* New York: Schocken, 1946.

Scott, R. B. Y. *Proverbs-Ecclesiastes.* Anchor Bible. New York: Doubleday, 1965.

Shauli, A. "Hasidic Legend and Aphorism as Literary Art Form." *Judaism* (Summer 1960) 229.

Sherman, Franklin. *The Promise of Heschel.* Philadelphia: J. B Lippincott, 1970.

Shook, L. K., ed. *Renewal of Religious Thought.* Montreal: Palm, 1968.

Sorokin, Pitirim A. *The Crisis of Our Age: The Social and Cultural Outlook.* New York: E. P. Dutton, 1957.

Spiegel, Shalom. *Hebrew Reborn.* Cleveland: Meridian, 1957.

Stace, Walter T. *Religion and the Modern Mind.* Philadelphia: J. B. Lippincott, 1960.

Talley, Eldon M. "The Wisdom of Heschel, review of *Man's Quest for God.*" *Cross Currents* (Summer 1966) 360.

Tillich, Paul. *Christianity and the Encounter of the World Religions.* New York: Columbia University Press, 1964.

Valera, Victor M. Perez. "Religious Experience in Abraham Joshua Heschel." *Journal of Service International de Documentation Judeo-Chretienne* 6:1 (1973) 4–9.

Walker, Thomas. *Jewish Views of Jesus: An Introduction and an Appreciation.* New York: Arno, 197.

Weinberg, Dudley. "The Efficacy of Prayer." In *Understanding Jewish Prayer*, edited by Jakob J. Petuchowski, 121–37. New York: Ktav, 1972.

Weiss-Rosmarin, Trude. "Who's Afraid of Dialogue." *Jewish Spectator* (May 1967) 25.

Whiston, Charles F. "Review of Heschel's *Man's Quest for God.*" *Religious Education* (Jul–Aug 1966) 315.

Wijnhoven, Jochanan H. A. "Gershon G. Scholem: The Study of Jewish Mysticism." *Judaism* (Fall 1970) 468–81.

Wolk, Samuel J. B. "Mysticism." In *The Universal Jewish Encyclopedia* 1:76. New York: Universal Jewish Encyclopedia, 1948.

Zelizer, Julian. *Abraham Joshua Heschel: A Life of Radical Amazement.* New Haven, CT: Yale University Press, 2021.